JN117746

POLAND
THE CENTENARY
OF REGAINING
INDEPENDENCE

On the Identity of Poles

International Scientific Conference on the Occasion
of the 100th Anniversary of Regaining Independence
of the Republic of Poland

Edited by:
Masahiro Taguchi

Forum Poland
Fukuro Shuppan

On the Identity of Poles

International Scientific Conference on the Occasion
of the 100th Anniversary of Regaining Independence
of the Republic of Poland

Edited by:
Masahiro Taguchi

Forum Poland
Fukuro Shuppan

Publisher: Fukuro Shuppan (Okayama, Japan)
Edited by: Masahiro Taguchi
Technical editing by: Filip Grądek
Conference organized by: Forum Poland
Conference co-organized by: Embassy of the Republic of
    Poland in Tokyo and Polish Institute in Tokyo

International Scientific Conference on the Occasion of the 100th Anniversary of Regaining Independence of the Republic of Poland "On the Identity of Poles"

Międzynarodowa Konferencja Naukowa z okazji Stulecia Odzyskania Niepodległości przez Rzeczpospolitą Polską "Wokół tożsamości Polaków"

This project is part of the commemoration of the centennial of the regaining of independence and rebuilding Polish statehood.

This publication was made possible through the support of Polish Institute In Tokyo.

POLAND
THE CENTENARY
OF REGAINING
INDEPENDENCE

Embassy
of the Republic of Poland
in Tokyo

ポーランド広報文化センター
POLISH INSTITUTE TOKYO

ISBN978-4-86186-784-2　C3030

Table of Contents

1. Program of the Conference

**International Scientific Conference on the Occasion of
the 100th Anniversary of Regaining Independence
of the Republic of Poland
"On the Identity of Poles"**

Date:
November 17th (Saturday) 2018, 10:00-16:00
Venue: Conference Hall, Building No. 1, Josai
University, Kioi-cho Campus
Organized by:
NPO Organizational Committee of Forum Poland
Co-organized by:
Embassy of the Republic of Poland in Tokyo,
Polish Institute in Tokyo

PROGRAM

9:30-10:00	Registration
	Moderator: Akiko Kasuya (Professor, Kyoto City University of Arts)
10:00-10:10	Welcome Speech: Jacek Izydorczyk (Ambassador of the Republic of Poland in Japan)
10:10-10:15	Welcome Speech: Masahiro Taguchi (Professor, Okayama University)
10:15-10:45	Keynote Lecture: Zdzisław Krasnodębski (Professor, University of Bremen)
10:45-11:00	Group photography
11:00-12:00	Keynote Lecture: Kumiko Haba (Professor, Aoyama Gakuin University)

2. Welcome Speech

Jacek Izydorczyk
(Ambassador of the Republic of Poland in Japan)

Ladies and gentlemen,

I am very pleased that I can give a welcome message at this conference. This year, Poland celebrates the 100th anniversary of regaining independence, and to celebrate this wonderful occasion, Polish diplomacy organizes many interesting events around the world. Today's conference is part of this series and I am convinced that it will be a very valuable contribution to the celebrations of the 100th anniversary, as well as to the debate and knowledge about contemporary Poland and Poles in Japan.

I thank the association and the organizing committee of the NPO Forum Polska, especially Prof. Masahiro Taguchi for cooperation and initiative in organizing this conference. I also thank the University of Josai for the possibility of organizing this event at this university, which has traditionally been involved in cooperation with the countries of Central Europe, including Poland.

Ladies and Gentlemen, I would especially like to welcome Mr. Zdzisław Krasnodębski, who is a special guest of this conference.

Due to the unique context and title of today's conference, it is worth mentioning some basic historical facts. The history of Poland is very rich. We have been counting our statehood since 966, the date of the Baptism of Poland, although certainly a strong state must have existed before. For centuries Poland was the most powerful, largest and richest country in Europe. Unfortunately, the sad, short part of Polish history is what is mainly known abroad, including Japan. Partitions in the eighteenth century, the Second World War, the period of communism.

After the partitions, on November 11, 1918, Poland became free thanks to the collective effort of the entire nation. So it has been 100 years and 6 days.

Poland is a great country, with inspiring history and great culture. Despite the distance of almost 10,000 kilometers, Poland and Japan have been joined by strong friendship for years. These ties are also strengthened by developing diplomatic relations, whose centennial anniversary will be celebrated in 2019.

I hope that today's conference will help to deepen knowledge and strengthen interests related to Poland in Japan. I wish you interesting presentations and discussions.

Thank you for your attention.

*At a conference at the University of Josai on 17/11/2018

3. Welcome Speech

Masahiro Taguchi
(Vice President of Forum Poland)

Thank you for attending the International Scientific Conference on the Occasion of the 100th Anniversary of Regaining Independence of the Republic of Poland "On the Identity of Poles". I would like to greet you on behalf of the Organizing Committee for Forum Poland, which will host this conference together with the Embassy of the Republic of Poland in Japan, and the Polish Institute in Tokyo.

The purpose of this conference is to discuss together with you the identity of Poles in modern Poland on the 100th anniversary of the recovery of Polish independence.

It is a great honor to welcome Professor Krasnodębski, a famous Polish sociologist. I want to welcome Professor Haba, a leading researcher on political and sociological problems of modern Central and Eastern Europe. I am very much looking forward to the keynote lectures of the two professors, who will analyze the 100 years of Poland from a global perspective. I would like to welcome distingushed researchers from various fields, who will give their special lectures. I expect heated discussions.

One keyword to think about contemporary Poland is "identity". Building an identity is not only the confirmation of one's values, but also the process of establishing a relationship with others. By tracing how the Polish identity has been inherited and changed, we can deepen our understanding of Poland and at the same time confirm the position and role of Poland in the world and Europe.

Polish identity is said to be multi-layered. There are identities rooted in the region, identities based on the sense of belonging to social groups, identities to the Polish state, identities as Europeans, identities to the Catholic world etc. And in various aspects, identities can be expressed in various ways or in a complex way. In this conference, lecturers will discuss about the identity of Poles from the fields of literature, language, economy, society and history.

Thank you for your attention.

4. 100 Years of Regaining of Independence and Polish Identity

Zdzisław Krasnodębski
(Professor, University of Bremen)

1. What is it that we celebrate?

In 2018 many nations in Europe celebrated their independence, gained in 1918 – Estonia, Latvia, Lithuania, Czech Republic. Even Georgians remembered with pride their short-lived independent Georgian Republic. Austrians and Germans, who belonged to the losers in WWI, also commemorated the founding of their first republics. The establishment of the Weimar Republic is now not considered as a result of catastrophe in national history, but as a positive act, what was stressed for the first time very strongly by President Steinmeier in his speech on the 9th of November 2018.

In Poland we celebrated 100 years of re-gaining the independence. Regaining - not achieving. This is an important difference. "Re-gaining" – because the independence of Poland lasted many centuries, not 100 years. Poland, as you know, has long history of statehood, going back to the tenth century. And there was never any deep and long break in the continuation of political and cultural existence, as can be observed in the history of many other nations in Europe, Czechs or Bulgarians for instance. Therefore it is a mistake to see the Polish history in the context of the late nation-building-processes in the second half of the 19th century, even if there were, of course, important changes in the self-perception and a scope of national consciousness during the 19th and 20th centuries and Poland after WWI was territorially and constitutionally different than it was before the partitions.

Even in these 123 years in which Poland was partitioned amongst its neighboring powers – Russia, Prussia and Austria – some forms of a Polish political entity existed. From 1807 until 1815 existed the Duchy of Warsaw, later the Vienna Congress re-established the Kingdom of Poland, with a personal Union with Russia, dependent on it, but with its own constitution, its own administration and army. This Polish army later fought against Russia in the November Uprising of 1830 – that was the last time in the 19th century that a regular Polish army was on the battlefields. In the January Uprising of 1863-65 there were only partisan units. Only in the last decades of the 19th century the so-called Polish Question, the idea of reestablishing Poland was removed from the European political agenda. Yet after 1867 the Polish language become the official language in the Austrian part of Poland, and Poles often took on high positions, as for instance the position of a prime minister of the Habsburg Empire.

Despite later political misfortunes, despite human losses, especially among the elites, Polish culture and Polish identity were preserved all this time, which makes Poles one of the most ancient nations in Europe. This continuity is astonishing. For instance, we can without great effort read and understand the poetry of Jan Kochanowski, who lived in the 16th century. There is no inventor, a father of Polish language, as in the case of many "belated" nations. Only recently we began to rediscover many aspects of the culture of the old Rzeczpospolita, for instance Polish religious and court music from the baroque period.

The celebrations in Eastern and Central Europe in 2018 show that WWI was not – at least not only – an unprecedented catastrophe of Europe – Urkatastrophe (original catastrophe) – as it is often described by historians, especially in Germany, and by contemporary politicians, especially in the European Union, and in its consequences a victory of nationalism in Europe that inevitably lead to its next tragic phase: WWII.

WWI was certainly a tragedy, it cost millions of human lives. But those commemorations of the end of the Great War also show that it led also to a liberation of nations and democratization of states. It is worth to remember that the Europe before 1914 was dominated by imperial powers, was not a paradise, and consisted it also of oppressed nations and persecuted, discriminated individuals.

Some historians, political scientists and politicians are inclined to neglect these facts. For instance, Christopher Clarke, the author of "Sleepwalkers", a famous work about the genesis of WWI, puts aside such facts and ignores the experiences of such a nation as Poland. As he stated in an interview for Frankfurter Allgemeine Zeitung:

"The First World War was the worst-case scenario for the beginning of 20th century.

The world of 1913, with its global trade, its cultural exchange, its peaceful changes, is shattered and wasted in a succession of disasters. You cannot imagine a worse start to the century. Stalinism with all its victims, Hitler, the Holocaust, the destruction of German cities in the air war: most of it can be traced back to the poison dose that this war has injected into Europe. It is a depressing prospect that we need all these wars and conflicts to produce renewal and change".[1]

In narrations of many nations in Central and Eastern Europe the atrocities of the war were less important than the fact of gaining national freedom and independence. As one historian writes with a tone of accusation: "For some post-imperial states – notably Poland, Czechoslovakia, and the Kingdom of Serbs, Croats and Slovenes (the future Yugoslavia) – a commemorative focus on the triumphal birth (or rebirth) of the nation state in 1918 enabled them to conveniently 'forget' that millions of their citizens had fought in the defeated armies of the Central Powers" .[2]

Is this really a surprise in the Polish case? Several generations strove to regain sovereignty, the loss of which meant that they could not be the host on their land, they were colonized and deprived of political and cultural rights. They fought for free Poland, and died for it. Some started to dream of a big war in Europe, as all dreams about solidarity of nations and of a political order based on a sense of justice turned out to be idealistic and naive. Unfortunately, a geopolitical order in Europe, in which there was place for Poland again, could be achieved only by that cruel war between the partioning countries, and not by negotiations with them or between them.

This sovereignty of Poland, regained in 1918, was short-lived – it lasted only twenty years. In 1939 Poland was unable to defend itself against two neo-imperial, revisionist states Nazi Germany and Soviet Russia. Poland rejected Hitler's demands, repeatedly put forward since autumn of

---

[1] Andreas Kilb, 'Gespräch mit dem Historiker Clark: Alle diese Staaten waren Bösewichte', *FAZ* 28.07.2014.
[2] Robert Gerwarth, *The Vanquished: Why the First World War Failed to End, 1917-1923*, Penguin Books Ltd. Kindle Edition, (Kindle Locations 299-301).

1938, and was attacked on September 1, 1939. Poland resisted but was quickly defeated in what was a seemingly true Blitzkrieg. Yet the fighting lasted until the beginning of October. The Polish government was evacuated, after the Soviet army invaded Poland on September 17, without declaring war. Until the end of the war, it functioned in exile. Poles continued fighting on the side of the Western Allies. It was in Poland that the greatest battle of the resistance movement in Europe took place – the 63-day Warsaw Uprising of 1944.

However, to regain real sovereignty Poland had to wait another four decades. For although the Polish People's Republic, established 1944/1945 was internationally acknowledged as a sovereign state, in reality it was controlled by Soviet Union – seizing and maintaining of power by communists in Poland would never be possible without Moscow's support. In 1989 we fully regained independence, after forty-fife years of communism, quite peacefully, without war or a bloody conflict.

2. Eternal victim?

From the perspective of all that has happened in modern times in Europe, we are inclined to look at Poland as an eternal victim of its neighbors. In such a pessimistic view, Poland is seen as always weak and as an object of aggression and occupation. There are of course historical reasons for such opinion: the partitions in the 18th century, the defeated uprisings, the terrible experiences of WWII, like the loss of almost 6 million citizens, the Holocaust, the extermination of the Polish intelligentsia, the almost complete destruction of Warsaw and – on the Soviet side –

deportations to Siberia and mass executions of Polish officers in Katyń and other places, post-war communist terror and repression. And apart from all that: a bitter feeling that the allies failed us – the conferences in Tehran and Yalta have to date remained a symbol of betrayal for Poles.

Yet this is a wrong historical presentism and a result of historical propaganda of neighboring powers, which for obvious reasons presented Poles as weak and not able to govern themselves. As Piotr Wandycz wrote: "In German and Russian textbooks, the country was presented as a historical failure. No wonder that the defense of the national heritage became an almost obsessive Polish concern".[3]

In any case, it is a historical fact that Polish Commonwealth had for a couple of centuries dominated East-Central Europe. In 1611 the Polish army occupied Moscow and Tsar Vasily IV Shuysky paid tribute to Polish king Sigismund III. Prussia was for a long time – until the mid-17th century – a fief of the Kingdom of Poland, some of its lands were an integral part of the Kingdom. At the end of the 17th century, in 1669, Poland was still able to defeat Russia, struggling at the same time with Sweden and the Cossacks, Brandenburg, and Transylvania. Chances to recover lost territories, like the Smoleńsk region from Russia, and to incorporate East Prussia into Poland were quite realistic under the reign of Jan Kazimierz and Jan Sobieski. Symptomatically the victory in Vienna by Sobieski in 1683 against Turkey is mentioned by Hegel as the only contribution of the Slavonic people to the progress of absolute spirit in history.

When Poland reemerged, it immediately became an

---

[3] Piotr S. Wandycz, 'Historiography of the Countries of Eastern Europe: Poland', *The American Historical Review*, Vol. 97, No. 4 (Oct., 1992), pp. 1011-1025.

important actor in eastern part of Europe. In 1920 the reborn
Poland was able to defend itself, and defend Europe against
the Red Army, which intended to spread communism
throughout Europe. Today Poland is the sixth largest
economy in the EU and strongest state in East-Central
Europe. This is why Russia views Poland as a serious
competitor in the region.

3. Loss of the Independence

Poles are, however, still haunted by the question, why
it came to the catastrophe at the end of the 18th century.
What was the reason for the decline of Rzeczpospolita?
Why did we lose sovereignty? [4]

Many historians and political thinkers blame the
internal organization of the Rzeczpospolita, of the
Commonwealth, its Republican character – the election of
the king and the role of the Sejm and sejmiki, the Diet and
local assemblies. As one historian writes, "Eighteenth-
century Poland was an object of bewilderment, if not

---

[4] Piotr Wandycz writes: "While Western historians of the Age of
Enlightenment- Voltaire, Montesquieu, or Gibbon would search for
the causes of the rise and decline of states, their Polish disciples
personally experienced the collapse of their state in the late
eighteenth-century   partitions   of   the   Polish-Lithuanian
Commonwealth. Thus, whether affected in terms of philosophy and
methodology of history, by the Enlightenment, Romanticism,
Positivism, Idealism, or Marxism, Polish historians could not escape
from the fact of the partitions. As a leading Polish scholar remarked
in 1923, "the fundamental question for our historiography has been to
fathom the understanding of the causes of Poland's fall." - Piotr S.
Wandycz, Historiography of the Countries of Eastern Europe: Poland,
The American Historical Review, Vol. 97, No. 4 (Oct., 1992), p. 1012.

contempt, to outside observers".[5] This was, however, a judgment from the point of the view of absolute monarchies of that time. From this perspective a special attachment of the Polish nobility to the citizen rights and responsibilities, their mistrust of royal power, their attachment to liberty and equality could be only a curiosity. Today our assessment of this republican system should be different.[6]

Others blamed not so much the political system itself as the Poles, Polish nobility, for its lack of unity, anarchy, internal quarrels and struggles. This was in the 18th century a wide-spread opinion about Poles. As Voltaire once said: "One Pole is a charmer; two Poles – a brawl; three Poles – well, this is the Polish Question".[7]

The third explanation stresses economic and social backwardness, the lagging behind the development of the West, neo-serfdom etc. In all three versions it had been, above all, internal reasons, Polish internal affairs, Poland's republican system, economy based on dominance of nobility, the Polish "national character" or mentality, which were considered the causes of the loss of sovereignty.

This is a never-ending discussion. And there will never be an ultimate answer. One has, however, to stress that self-blaming ignores the change of the geopolitical situation, on which Poland did not have a big influence. In his famous essay first published in 1833 "Die großen Mächte" Leopold

---

[5] Jerzy Lukowski, Political Ideas among the Polish Nobility in the Eighteenth Century (To 1788) *The Slavonic and East European Review*, Vol. 82, No. 1 (Jan., 2004), pp. 1-26.
[6] Anna Grześkowiak-Krwawicz, *Dyskurs polityczny Rzeczypospolitej Obojga Narodów*, Wydawnictwo Naukowe Uniwersytetu Mikołaja Kopernika, Toruń 2018.
[7] quoted in Davies, Norman, *Europe: A History*. Oxford University Press, Oxford 1996.

von Ranke argued that is was above all the diminishing of
French influence in Eastern Europe and Russian victory
over Sweden that doomed Poland. In this epoch some old
powers, such as Spain, Turkey and Poland plunged into
crisis, while England, Russia, and Prussia emerged.
Together with Austria and France they dominated Europe in
19th century.[8]

It is not accidental that Poland regained its sovereignty
when the geopolitical situation in this part of Europe had
again changed fundamentally, because of the defeat of the
Central Powers and the Bolsheviki's coup d'état in Russia.
Discussions about the reason of partitions, about the sense
of the military struggle for independence, are continued
alongside the current discussions about the loss of the
Second Republic, about Polish foreign policy directly
before WWII, about the Warsaw Uprising of 1944.

4. Changing fate and perseverance

Modern Polish national identity is shaped by that
experience of that changing fate. Polish politics and public
life are full of historical analogies and metaphors. Memory
of the past glory and the past defeat and suffering – the loss
of the I Rzeczpospolita, uprisings in the 19th century, the
invasion by Nazi Germany and the Soviet Union in 1939,
Nazi and Communist terror, Communist dominance in
Poland and, despite all of that, resilience and perseverance.
Winston Churchill was right, when he said in the House of
Commons on the 1 October 1939:

---

[8] Die grossen Mächte, in: *Preussische Geschichte*, Emil Vollmer
Verlag, Essen, n. d., s. 11 -37, cf. 20-21.

"The soul of Poland is indestructible... she will rise again as a rock, which may for a spell be submerged by a tidal wave, but which remains a rock".[9]

This identity is also shaped by an ambivalent attitude towards the West – aspiration and feeling of inferiority, because of differences in economic development. Once this belonging to the West meant, above all, a common religion. As Józef Szujski, the founder of the Cracow historians' school wrote: "With Roman Catholic religion Poland has become a citizen of the West. This citizenship meant sharing its interests, serving its ideas and being be educated under his influence".[10] Today – in the eyes of many left-wing and liberal politicians, both in Poland and in the UE – it is religion that isolates Poland in the West.

Szujski formulates also the thesis that Poland compared with the West is younger in terms of civilization (młodszość cywilizacyjna). Most importantly, however, for that feeling of 'not being totally Western' were economic differences and the sense of having remained behind the West in terms of development. The ambivalent relation to "the West" still influences Poland's foreign policy.[11]

Interestingly, in the time of Solidarność (1980-81) it was Japan that became a symbol of success and a model of future development of Poland. The leader of Solidarność, Lech Wałęsa announced at that time that Poland soon would be "the second Japan". This was one of the rare moments,

---

[9] Quoted in Churchill, Winston Spencer (2005). *Maxims and Reflections*. Kessinger Publishing.
[10] Józef Szujski, 'Rzut oka na stanowisko Polski w historii powszechnej', in: Józef Szujski, *O fałszywej historii jako mistrzyni fałszywej polityki*, PIW, Warszawa 1991, pp. 23-66, quotation p.28.
[11] Cf. Molly Krasnodębska, 'Politics of Stigmatization: Poland as a "Latecomer"', in the *European Union*, forthcaming.

in which not any of the leading countries of the West, but an Asian country was a kind of benchmark for Poles.

5. Back to Europe

Since 1989 Poland is back in Europe, and a part of "the West". It is a member of NATO and the EU, it is making up for the time lost during the communist period, catching up economically and politically. Poles are looking to the future with great hope and more confidence. Some are speaking with a bit of exaggeration about a new golden age of Poland.

It is true that the gap between Poland and the most developed Western parts of the continent is gradually diminishing. This does not mean that old dangers and concerns have completely disappeared. Russia once again has become a threat for all of Europe but especially for its neighboring countries. There are other – softer – threats, such as political pressure, economic dependency and attempts of cultural control, coming from our Western partners, above all Germany and the EU- institutions, which it dominates. Some tendencies, as ideas expressed, for instance, by the French president, are causing concern throughout Europe.

In internal Polish politics and public life we see a lot of continuation of old patterns of behavior. It is not the democracy that is the problem, but some traits of political life in Poland – as always full of exaggerated emotions, extreme opinions and inclination to appeal to foreign powers to engage in our internal affairs. Notwithstanding all problems the Third Republic already exists more than ten years longer than the Second Republic and Poland is now regaining not its sovereignty but, step by step the status in

Europe it once had. We hope that Poland has at last escaped from the cycle of those dramatic changes of political fortune, which so affected the previous generations.

5. 100th Anniversary of Polish Independence

Power Transition and the 100 years after
the Great War - the Declining Great Powers
and Reconstructing the New World Order

Kumiko Haba
(Professor, Aoyama Gakuin University)

1. Symptoms of War and Power Transition

It is an honor to have a presentation on the 100-year Anniversary of Polish Independence. At present, the role of Poland in the world as a member and leader of the EU seems to be continuously growing.

Currently, as 100 years have passed since the end of World War I and with conflicts and nationalism occurring frequently around the world, we need to investigate and learn from the history of the past 100 years, analyzing what happened using the sharpened intellectual tools and spirit.

UK's 2016 referendum for withdrawal from the EU and the election of President Donald Trump, the sentiment for "Strong America" and nationalism, have revealed a new era of "Post-Truth" and "anti-intellectualism" of Europe, especially the UK, and the USA, the Anglo-Saxon Great Power of the 20th century.

The spread of "home country-focused" populism and antagonism in Europe and the USA, as well as the trends of exclusion of others seem to have a strong resemblance with the start of World War I.

The biggest and most terrible common characteristic is that a "relatively long peace" has continued and the "generations who do not know war" have become a majority in the society.

At the outbreak of World War I, young people went to war waving their hands with joy and laughter, as if they were going on a trip. But what awaited them was a prolonged war and a massive death toll of young people.

In the eve of the First World War nationalism was on the rise, conflicts and clashes at the borders occurred, and the inevitable consequence was the outbreak of war arising from accidental events.

The war was prolonged and many citizens were sacrificed as a result of the improved technologies used in the conflict. On the other hand, ethnic and social revolutions broke out in various places, including the independence movements of Serbia and Bosnia, which directly triggered the war, and the four Great Powers; the Russian, German, Habsburg and Ottoman Empires all collapsed and many independent emerging nations were born.

In Russia the Democratic Revolution and the Socialist Revolution happened subsequently, and the Soviet Union they brought about lasted for more than 70 years as a socialist regime, but failed to achieve the symbolic 100 years of continuity in history and collapsed.

The socialist revolutions that occurred in Central and Eastern Europe were crushed but the ethnic revolutions survived. Four Empires collapsed from the inside, forming the basis for a "nation-states system" and "sovereign states system" in the 20th century. This was supported by the independence of various ethnic states in Central and Eastern Europe.

However, the formation of the "nation-states" and the subsequent destabilization soon gave rise to irredentism of the defeated countries, and as a result, people started a new war to correct borders again after 20 years. The whole of Europe became a battlefield, the land was left completely devastated and more than 50 million people lost their lives in Europe and Asia.

"War is a zero-sum game". Winners take territory, losers lose it. However, those who had lost territory will no doubt continue to hold grudges, even for hundreds of years and prepare for a war to regain them. There is no end to the war over territory.

After the Second World War, in the midst of devastation and scorched earth, Europeans vowed that they would never again start a war in the name of their territory and national interests. And so, going beyond the nation-state, the history of European integration has begun.

But now, Europe and the world are shaking between the populism and nationalism of "home country first", and the joint regional movement. One example is the United Kingdom, which is experiencing this "shaking" as it leaves the EU. Interestingly, developed countries such as the UK and the USA, who had led the free trade system in the 20th century, have turned inward with protecting their "own country first", while on the other hand, the emerging superpowers such as China, India and ASEAN have been advocating regional collaboration, such as the Belt and Road Initiative (BRI), the South Asian Association for Regional Cooperation (SAARC) and BIMSTEC. They are embarking on the path of cooperation with the world, with other the countries belonging to BRICS and the AU (African Union) and with other developing regions around the globe.

History is just like the Chinese proverb and story about

the old man who lost his horse: good and bad things in life alternate unpredictably, luck and misfortune come twisted together like strands in a rope.

Historically, federations, nation-states, and regional integration (unions) emerged repeatedly. Politically, there is no conclusion as to which is better: the nation state or a federation, protectionism or regional collaboration. However, it is also clear from history that nationalism stemming from protectionism and "home country first" approach has caused regional instability, and that various types of increasing friction are likely to create conflict and war crises.

The fall of the Habsburg Empire brought the independence of Poland, Czechoslovakia, Hungary and Yugoslavia, but after these countries gained sovereignty, instability continued in Central and Eastern Europe between the menace of the Soviet Union's socialist regime and the irredentism of Germany, Italy and Hungary. That made inevitable the need for stronger states and stability. Regional cooperation at first, then the autocracy and military governments, and at last the crisis of conflicts and wars. It has, therefore, brought inevitably the next World War. The subsequence of events in history gives us many lessons.

We are at a historical turning point of the world: it has been a 100 years since the end of the First World War, 80 years since the end of the Second World War, and 30 years since the Cold War came to a halt. We can now say that it depends on us all, on the young people in the 21st century, and on constructing a farseeing international community, to find out how to build a future of stability and prosperity.

As it seems that the war crisis and instability are approaching again with populism and protectionism of today, we are faced with a difficult task of steering away from war and conflicts, and creating a new era at the turning point of the history without destroying our mutual interests.

As a researcher concerned with regional integration, I would like us to look at the events of the last 100 years together and consider what should be done to maintain peace and rebuild the world order during historically unstable times.

2. Modernization and War

The "Democratic Peace" theory, based on the analysis of statistics of wars, which says that "Democracies never (or almost never) go to war against each other"[1] was used as a justification for President George Bush Jr. to start the war in Iraq.

In contrast to this, the famous linguist Noam Chomsky, when writing on the topic of 9/11, criticized the United States as the most "torturing democracy" and a "terrorist state" (Chomsky [2002]).

Even before Bruce Russett's analysis, it was generally believed that thanks to modernization and democratization the "barbaric" dictatorships vanished, and people achieved peace and prosperity. Historically speaking, modern civilization certainly made people richer and happier. But on the other hand, as a result of the recent postcolonialism we have advanced our research on the atrocities inflicted upon the indigenous people as a result of colonization with the inventions and discoveries of modern science and technology. Numerous new studies are also revealing that

---

[1] For more information on Democratic Peace Theory, see Russet [1996].

the war with modern heavy weapons has expanded and cruelized armed conflicts beyond comparison with the Middle Ages. The escalation of cruelty of wars has been becoming evident in the new researches.

The invention of "matchlock, navigation, and compass" in the course of modernization contributed to the fact that the modern nations discovered, pioneered, and developed all around the world, but also brought invasion, wars and colonization (Diamond [2005]).

In the First World War, the invention of the technology of flight and of the fighter aircraft expanded the war from a traditional two-dimensional framework to three dimensions, causing a great deal of damage in the war not only at the front lines but also to civilians.

The development of tanks and other heavy weapons in the WWII, nuclear weapons at the end of the war, and the development of chemical weapons in the Vietnam war - all these technologies made it possible to harm and kill human beings on a much larger scale and to expand the damage so dramatically, that during the Cold War it invited the fear of a possibility of Earth destruction.

In its early days, modernization brought development of weapons and warcraft, thus leading to brutalization of war. It is crucial that we take responsibility and keep asking questions about the resulting reality of tremendous sacrifices among the civilians at the backstage of the conflicts (Masukawa [2015], Ikeuchi [2016]).

The cruelties of the "totalitarian state" are countless. However, they too are a product of modernization and it is necessary to face the fact that nuclear development, intercontinental ballistic missiles around the globe, and remote-controlled drones can cause massive slaughters and are capable of destroying our world. With modern technology that can destroy the Earth and mankind, we can no longer have a world war.

Even after the end of the Cold War, people did not stop waging war and producing weapons under the pretense of the expanding regional conflicts, but turned to anthrax bacteria, cyber warfare and drones – advanced technologies which enable a so-called "clean war" through remote control of the conflict. All this has happened amidst our everyday life.

Even though Newsweek and others have repeatedly reported that the US soldiers could not handle this mentally, consequently suffering from an increase in mental illness and suicide rates (Newsweek [2012], Watanabe [2016]), people have not stopped inventions that simplify killing other people on an even larger scale, calling that a "defense" against the threat of terrorism and war.

There is no doubt that the scientific inventions of democratic countries have improved the deadly technologies year after year (Ikeuchi, Kodera, eds. [2016]). It is not only the emerging and "barbaric" nations that have cruelized and refined warfare. We need to take a straight look at the latest scientific and technological developments of modernization.

<Anti-Intellectualism, Post-Truth and War>
Amid the widening inequality and the influx of immigrant refugees due to globalization, Great Britain and the United States, the two major victorious powers and champions of modern democracy, are waving the flag of Britain-First and America-First nationalism, protectionism and unconcealed rejection of others. They have begun to take actions that go against the common sense of modern liberalism and democracy. European countries are no

exception, and far-right exclusionism is sweeping across Europe and the Americas.

As the words of these times: "post-truth" and "anti-intellectualism" indicate, an era has emerged in which the middle-class, which has traditionally supported the "common sense" of the modern nation-state, has overturned its practical wisdom.[2] It has emerged from the two great nations – symbols of modernization – reaching their economic peak and from nationalism.

Where is the cause of this?

In the 1930s, the late capitalist countries that pursued the developed nations created populism and dictatorship with the help of their enthusiastic people.

In the modern world, the advanced countries and leaders of modernization, such as Britain and the United States, amid the sense of crisis of being overtaken by the developing countries and with the help of populism, are becoming exclusive, anti-intellectual and aggressive. Why?

In Europe, there is an elderly part of population that has experienced the devastation of war and feels an imperative to evade it, as well rural and low-income populations – a broad segment of classes that wants to protect the welfare state (from immigration), put restrictions on migrants and refugees. This presents the welfare nationalism and xenophobia, along with the obscured American and European segregationalism.

Economic pressure is in the background of this. The economic crisis of the developed countries is obvious.

---

[2] For Post Truth and Counter-intellectualism: Davis [2018], D'Ancona [2017], Morimoto [2015], Uchida, Akasaka, Odajima [2015].

Table 1 World Economic Growth Rate in by country 2016
(190 countries)

Developing Powers			Developed Powers	
1.	Iran	10.3%	...	
2.	Iraq	10.0%	128. United Kingdom	1.8%
3.	Ethiopia	8.0%	129. Germany	1.8%
4.	Uzbekistan	7.8%	131. United States	1.6%
5.	Ivory Coast	7.5%	...	
6.	Iceland	7.2%	148. France	1.23%
7.	Cambodia	7.0%	...	
8.	Laos	6.9%	...	
9.	Bangladesh	6.9%	155. Japan	0.999%
10.	Tajikistan	6.9%	...	
11.	Philippines	6.8%	169. Russia	-0.225%
12.	India	6.8%	189. (South Sudan)	-13.8%
13.	China	6.7%	190. (Venezuela)	-18.0%

Source: IMF [2017].

Looking at world economic growth rate in 2016, (announced in 2017), China and India are included among the top of the countries with the highest economic growth rate, alongside other small and medium-sized countries. On the other hand, near the bottom of the growth rate table are the advanced powers of the United States, Britain, Germany, France and Japan.

Such is the current economic situation in the world and in the developed countries. And this is the cause of social instability and "post-truth". Where are we heading? How to stop this?

3. The World War: the Collapse of the Great Powers and the Formation of a New Order

As the American political scientist A.F.K. Organski and Harvard professor Graham Allison showed in their books - *World Politics* (Organski [1968]) and *Destined for war* (Alison [2017]) – changes in international power relations can cause insecurity, tension, and friction within developed countries, and these are often settled by war, as a result of which the developing nations emerge victorious and preach the start of a new international order.[3] This depiction bears an eerie resemblance to the contemporary situation.

World War I started under circumstances just like the described above. It began when a young Bosnian Serb, and a member of Yugoslav nationalist group "Young Bosnia", Gabrillo Prinzip, "accidentally" assassinated Archduke Franz Ferdinand, the heir to the Habsburg Empire. The Emperor Franz Joseph I of Austria declared war against Serbia after posing an unacceptable ultimatum. In response, in a short time most of the European countries got involved in the armed conflict, in a chain reaction which was tied to the power balance at that time. And so, a small assassination incident in a frontier area triggered a major conflict – a Great War in Europe and in Asia as well.

At first, no one thought that the empire would collapse from the initially small conflict. The Emperor and government of the Habsburg Empire predicted that it would likely be over within several weeks or by that year's Christmas at most, but the war continued for almost four and

---

[3] This is an example that is often cited as "Thucydides' trap" in international politics: Thucydides [2013].

half years, and the loser was not Serbia, but the Habsburg Monarchy, which ultimately collapsed not due to war, but by itself, its inside revolutionary movements, and by the will of independence of its nations.

All of four Empires which ruled over Europe were undone in the First World War, starting with the collapse of the Russian Empire by the outbreak of the Russian Revolution, German Empire by the November Revolution, the Habsburg Empire by the independence movement and declaration of independence by its minority nations, and at last, the Ottoman Empire by the Young Turk Revolution and the Arab Revolt. They were not destroyed in war, but by themselves from the inside, one after another. Nation-states were born and established as their "successor states" as the effect of nationalist independence movements and the endeavors of their leaders.

From the fall of the four empires, the new, sovereign nation-states were born. Their independence, however, caused new territorial anxiety and conflicts among the nations, and before long, irredentism surfaced, especially in the claims of Germany and Italy, and after short 20 years of crisis, a new war broke out in 1939, 80 years ago from 2019.

In defeated Germany, the democratic Weimar Republic was established after World War I, but Germany suffered from having to pay high war reparations and a worsening economy. As a result, the Nazi Party rose to power as the ruling party through general election, formed its government, and before long the German Army marched to the East, to gain the "living space". At first Germany annexed Sudetenland and soon it invaded and occupied Poland as well. Subsequently, the Nazi Germany established the notorious concentration camp in Auschwitz and Birkenau. Under the German occupation, more than a million people were sent to a terrible death one after another: Jews, Poles, Roma, as well as the mentally challenged, homosexuals and Soviet prisoners of war.

Eventually, German Nazism and Italian Fascism were overthrown by the combined effort of the Allied Forces, especially the Soviet Union's Red Army, and the partisan movements in various parts of the world.

<Cold War after World War II>

The Cold War started with the Soviet Army in Eastern Europe on one side, and NATO (from 1949) in Western Europe, especially in West Germany on the other side. Under such occupation of the Soviet Army and Warsaw Treaty Organization (from 1955), the East European movement for independence and sovereignty continued, with the East German uprising of 1953, the Polish independence movements, the Hungarian Revolution of 1956, and the Solidarity movement in Poland through the 1980s.

Finally, Perestroika and democratization of the Soviet Union also started in 1985, parallel to the Eastern and Central European cultural movements in the 1980s, and revolutions in the Eastern Bloc occurred one after another, opening the Iron Curtain: the Solidarity movement, the "Pan European Picnic", the Velvet Revolution in Czechoslovakia, the Fall of Berlin Wall, and the Romanian Revolution and execution of Nicolae Ceaușescu.

Because of its "twin deficits", the United States also sought compromise with the Soviet Union, and both US and the USSR finally met and announced the end of the Cold War, in December 1989. Before that, the "Revolutionary Dominoes" occurred in which East European states became independent from the Soviet Union one after another, the

Soviet-Eastern European socialist system collapsed at the end of 1989, and at last the fall of the Soviet Union continued in December 1991. The Communist-Socialist System that began with the Russian Revolution did not last and collapsed in only about 70 years, not passing the symbolic mark of a 100 years in history.

Until now the mankind failed to learn from its history and to conceive a way of changing the international order other than through revolution and war.

But the present times, when nuclear missiles are scattered all over the world, even in North Korea, are an opportunity for our kind to peacefully carry out official diplomacy and talks, achieve global and regional stability and prosperity through economic development and change power relations without going through wars and conflicts. I strongly believe that the human race is not stupid enough to go on the path of wrath and ruin the world.

After two thousand years of repeated territorial conflicts and becoming a stage of two great wars, Europe has established a system based on regional integration, in which there has not been a war in more than 70 years after WWII, at least where it has been in place. Are we able to turn it into a world-wide system?

Is it not possible to create an order change not through war and military power but rather through reconciliation, economic cooperation, and institution-building?

4. The collapse of Empires and the rise of nationalism

100 years ago, a global conflict called the First World War brought the downfall of four European empires, from

which a new order and new nation states were formed. It was then that Central and Eastern European countries were born (or re-born), such as Poland, Czechoslovakia, Hungary, Yugoslavia, Romania and Bulgaria.

When great powers such as Russian, German, Habsburg and Ottoman empires – the empires that symbolized the Early and Late Modern Period Europe, collapsed in the course of the war, the leaders of nations such as Poland formed their respective nation-states (Haba [1991]).

In the view of historical realism there is no "if" in history, and the events that occurred, even if as a result of a plot, are deemed inevitable. If we look at it this way, then the contradictory events of the failure of the Socialist Revolution in Central and Eastern Europe in 1918 and the success of the national independence movements on one hand, and the Russian short-lived Democratic Revolution, the success of Socialist Revolution, and the collapse of the Soviet Union after 70 years on the other – they all bear vital implications when analyzed in the context of subsequent history (Hobsbawm [1996]).

After the Second World War, why did the Eastern European Socialist regimes, implemented by the expanding influence of the Soviet Union, collapse so rapidly, even though the system lasted for nearly half a century?

Why did people of Central and Eastern Europe, notably in Poland, happily escape from the Soviet rule as soon as the opportunity came and promptly joined the NATO in order not to come under the Soviet military influence ever again? When we think about the last hundred years of Polish and European history, and consider how the two World Wars and the Cold War affected the Polish people, we might learn a valuable lesson from knowing how they look at the history of their country and the world themselves. It is a lesson of the importance of nation's sovereignty and independence, of a historical and fundamental vigilance against Russia and about solidarity with the West, even if it is betrayed.

We can write new pages of history only if we learn from these painful experiences, no matter what part of the world we are in.

5. The end of World War I and the search for a new order

In the course of the outbreak and the end of World War I, the trends in national and regional restructuring, which have significantly affected international and national politics even to the present day, are threefold: the federal system, the nation-state and regional integration.

<1. Attempts to (re)organize the federal state e.g. The Danubian Federation>

The first one is a historical attempt at federal re-organization. In the late 19th century, the idea of reorganizing the declining powers into a variety of federal regimes gained popularity due to the rise of nationalism and the growing influence of regionalism. Efforts at creating a federal system appeared repeatedly in the late 19th and the early 20th centuries, proposed as a program for the federalization of the Habsburg Empire.

After the 1848-49 Hungarian Revolution and War of Independence was quenched, the Danubian Federation (or Confederation) concept was brought forward by Lajos Kossuth. It was an attempt to transform the ethnic tensions into multi-ethnic, multi-regional coexistence (Haba [1994-

2004]). After the Austro-Hungarian Compromise the initiative faded for a moment, but re-emerged in between the end of the 19th and the beginning of the 20th century, taking on the forms of The United States of Greater Austria, The Balkan Federation, The Central-European Federation – a continuous history of ideas, all of them being different concepts reshaping the Habsburg Empire, making up a major trend together with the theory of "Mitteleuropa". However, the Empire was dismantled as a result of the rise of national movements, while the idea of federalization could not withstand historical trials, and modern nation-states were then formed.

<2. Modern nation-state formation>
  The second is an attempt to form a modern nation-state. Shortly after the war, the countries of Central and Eastern Europe that emerged in between Germany and Russia and a collection of small states, unstable politically and economically, that could not be united (Mayer [1983]). As a result, they were either gradually dismantled in the '30s or moved towards dictatorship and were incorporated into the spheres of influence of their neighboring powers, such as Germany and Russia.

  These nation-states "squeezed between" the great powers were indeed so fragile that one after another they shifted to authoritarian dictatorship, as described in Anthony Polonsky's *Little dictators* (Polonski [1993]). Later, these countries were either re-annexed or used by Germany and Soviet Union – the inheritors of the former empires.

  Which is more preferable for people living in Central and Eastern Europe, a federal state or a nation-state? This is also a major dilemma in the restructuring of multi-ethnic nations that continues to this day, however, today's tendencies towards nationalism are stronger than those towards federalism.

After the end of the Cold War, Yugoslavia, Czechoslovakia, and the Soviet Union, as a result of democratization, turned to the direction of dissolution of federal states, as a result of their democratization. Conflicts continued especially in Yugoslavia from 1991 to 1999, with massacres that prompted NATO intervention and bombings in Bosnia (1995) and Kosovo (1999).

The characteristic trend was, in order to ensure national and regional stability, to quickly turn to either the EU, NATO, the Visegrád Group or CIS, and thus having maintained sovereignty, to seek regional cooperation and restructuring.

<3. Regional collaboration and regional integration>

The reflection that came as a result of the two World Wars took the form of the attempt at regional integration and regional cooperation, after the formation of small, sovereign nation-states.

After the Second World War, in order to restrain Germany, which had scarred Europe with war and the Holocaust, the country was divided and incorporated into the new political order. Not long after, the German-French 'reconciliation' became a fact and the movement towards European integration began, with a war-free Europe as its goal.

The post-war regional integration, however, was not intended to include Germany, which bore the biggest responsibility for the war in Europe, but instead to rule out the Soviet Union which had brought the victory of Allied countries by leading Great Patriotic War that drove away the German forces at the end of World War II. Post-war regional integration was formed excluding the Soviet Union and encompassing Germany, which caused the war. The same is true in the Far East. The new order in the Far East was formed with the inclusion of a defeated axis country – Japan and excluding China, one of the winning side nations, as it turned towards Socialism.

Ideologically motivated hostility and exclusion of Russia and China have been preserved until today.

Epilogue: Towards the new international order. War or prosperity?

The era in which the emerging Asian economies like China and India are surpassing the developed powers of the 20th century, such as the United States, Europe, and Japan is at our doorstep. However, the movement towards building a new system in terms of international order and value has not yet begun. That is why the developed economies of both Europe and the United States should, rather than unnecessarily amplifying nationalism and aggravating divisions, avoid the dangers of conflict and war and think about the shape of a new international order that includes the developing nations of Asia, Africa and Latin America.

As the tasks of international politics are now at the turning point of a major historical era, to avoid the "order change due to war" between the emerging nations and the superpowers, as described by Organski and Alison, we need to examine, verify and then implement a peaceful and stable way of achieving that transition and building a new system.

At this point in history, with the new wave of global

changes that are coming after the two World Wars and a Cold War that have shaped the world order as we know it, our biggest concern is how to reconstitute this order, not through a new war, but on the basis of peace, prosperity, sovereignty, regional and world-wide collaboration, with the joint wisdom of different nations, for their mutual benefit.

References

Allison, Graham [2017]. *Destined for War: Can America and China Escape Thucydides's Trap?,* Houghton Mifflin Harcourt.

Chomsky, Noam [2002], *9.11. – Not Eligible to Retaliate to America!* (Japanese) Bungeishunju, Tokyo.

D'Ancona, Matthew [2017]. *Post-Truth: The New War on Truth and How to Fight Back,* Ebury Press.

Davis, Evan [2018]. *Post-Truth: Peak Bullshit - and What We Can Do About It*, Abacus.

Diamond, Jared [2005]. Translated by Akira Kurahone, *Guns, Germs, and Steel: The Fates of Human Societies,* Norton, New York.

Haba, Kumiko (eds.) [1991]. *Russian Revolution and Eastern Europe,* Sairyusha.

Haba, Kumiko [1994 (first ed.)-2004 (seventh ed.)]. *Nationality Question of Integrated Europe,* Kodansha.

Haba, Kumiko [2014a]. 'Power Shift—National Anxiety, Territorial Dispute and Xenophobia', *Academic Tendency*, Science Council of Japan, January.

Haba, Kumiko [2014b]. *Asian Regional Integration in the Global Era,* Iwanami Shoten, 2012. Chinese Translation.

Haba, Kumiko [2016a]. *Division and Integration in Europe; Nationalism and Borders in Enlarged EU - Inclusion or Exclusion*, Chuokoron-Shinsha, Tokyo.

Haba, Kumiko [2016b]. *Division and Integration of Europe*, Chuokoron-Shinsha.

Haba, Kumiko [2017a]. 'War, Declining Great Power and Reorganization of the World Order-100 years of Russian Revolution', *Arena*, Vol .20.

Haba, Kumiko [2017b]. *Considering Asian Regional Integration—How to avoid war*, Akashi Shoten.

Hirschfeld, Gerhard (ed.) [2012]. *Brill's Encyclopedia of the First World War*, (2 Vols), Brill, Leiden & Boston.

Hobsbawm, Eric (translated by Hidekazu Kawai) [1996]. *The Age of Extremes: The Short Twentieth Century, 1914–1991*, Sanseido.

Ikeuchi, Satoru [2016]. *Scientists and War*, Iwanami Shoten.

IMF [2017]. World Economic Outlook Databases April, 2017.

Kibata, Yoichi [2012]. 'First World War as a Total War', *War in 20th Century*, Yushisha.

Maddison, Angus [2007a]. *Contours of the world Economy, 1-2030 AD; Essays in Macroeconomic History*, Oxford University Press, September.

Maddison, Angus [2007b]. *Chinese Economic Performance in the Long Run, 960-2030*, OECD, Paris, October.

Masukawa, Toshihide [1983]. *What Scientists Do in War*, Shueisha, 2015.

Mayer, A.J. (translated by Yoichi Kibata and Takashi Saito), *Wilson vs. Lenin <1> - political origin 1917- 1918*, Iwanami Shoten.

Morimoto, Anri [2015]. *Anti-intellectualism: the identity of the "fever" that America created*, Shinchosha.

Newsweek [2016]. "The cry of a young American soldier

who commits suicide after returning" *Newsweek*, 2012.8.7.

Organski, A.F.K. [1968]. *World Politics*, Alfred A. Knopf.

Polonski, Antony [1993]. Translated by Kumiko Haba et al. *Little Dictators*, Hosei University Press.

Russett, Bruce (translated by Takehiko Kamo) [1996], *Pax Democratia, Principles for the World after the Cold War,* University of Tokyo Press.

Thucydides, (translated by Haruo Konishi) [2013]. *Thucydides' History,* Chikuma Shoten.

Toffler, Alvin [1990]. *Power Shift; Knowledge, Wealth, and Violence at the Edge of the 21st century.*

Uchida, Tatsuru, Mari Akasaka, Takashi Odajima [2015]. *Anti-Intellectualism in Japanese Society*, Shobunsha.

Watanabe, Yukari [2016]. 'Why soldiers who survived the battlefield collapse in the US', *Newsweek*, 2016.8.31.

Yamamuro, Shin-ichi [2014]. *First World War,* Vol 1. Iwanami Shoten.

6. On the Identity of the "Émigré-writer" Leon Gomolicki

Hikaru Ogura

(Assistant professor, Toyo University)

Introduction

The main subject of this paper is Russian diaspora in interwar Poland, and one writer who underwent a transformation that changed him from a Russian exile to a Pole. "Russian diaspora" might seem as a strange topic at the International Conference on the 100th anniversary of Poland's Independence, but it is an attempt to use the reversed perspective of a stranger, an exile, to shed some light on the country that accepted him.

A wealth of research has accumulated on Russian exile cultures in Paris, France, Berlin, Germany, Prague, the Czech Republic, Harbin, China, and Beograd, Serbia, which originated with the wave of massive emigration caused by the Russian revolution and Civil War. The Polish Russian diaspora, on the other hand, has not been addressed enough in the existing literature. This particular diaspora community, although by no means small in its overall size, was generally strongly political in nature, making it difficult to observe its cultural developments. Among other things, there were few famous representatives of its culture and literature. Gippius and Merezhkovsky, famous poets, left Russia at the end of 1919 and arrived in Warsaw after they had traveled through Minsk and Vilnius. In October 1920,

in the wake of the Polish government's ceasefire
negotiations with Bolsheviks, they moved on to Paris and
never returned to Poland and thus could not offer
observations about the Russian exile culture there.

1. Polish anti-Russian sentiment

An article from 1921 and published in Berlin, in
journal "Russkaia kniga" (Русская книга), tells us that very
few Russian language books were published in Poland
during this time.

Poland is the only city in Europe where three-quarters
of the population know Russian. The number of Russian
exiles in Poland presumably reaches hundreds of
thousands. It would seem that the best conditions for the
development of the publishing business are met.
However, Russian publications in Poland are in fact in a
situation where the few newspapers disappear as soon as
they are issued. Russian books are fewer than in any
other European country. The reasons for this situation
are varied. The decades of emperor's repressions have
caused aversion to everything that has Russian
characteristics – this is still not a story of the past. […]
Even among the Russian expatriates, the publications are
not selling well. And there is no "Russian diaspora" in
Poland in the true sense of the word. There are only
"refugees". People who got caught in the waves of the
events and were thrown out of the Soviet Russia to
wherever they could go ended up in Poland only because
it was close to them. […] That is why in Poland today
you can publish only books that do not have to bring

profit, such as political brochures.[1]

In addition to Polish anti-Russian sentiments, the difficult situation of Russian "refugees" in Poland made it very difficult for Russian publication to grow and flourish. This contrasts with the publishing situation of Russian books in Berlin which was at this same time, the "capital of Russian literature", and surpassed even, Moscow and Petersburg.

Nevertheless, during the interwar period after Poland regained independence, there were several literary groups in the Polish Russian diaspora that were quite active. Publishers and literary circles frequently held readings and lectures in Warsaw, Vilnius, Lvov, Cracow, Grodno, Rivne and other cities.

While the market for Russian literature in Poland may have been anemic, Polish literature has long functioned as a "window to the West" for Russia (e.g., in Russia there was a high demand for the works of Mickiewicz from the end of the 19th to the beginning of the 20th century). During the interwar period, when it became impossible to freely enjoy Polish literature in the Soviet Union, Russians exiles, who had access to Polish literature, received it positively and tried to reflect it in their own texts. As an example, Belgrade, which belongs to the same Slavic-languages circle, was not politically antagonized with Russia, and what is more, shared the same Orthodox Christian faith, can be pointed to as having close ties with Russia as a recipient of refugees. However, rather than observing big impact of Yugoslavian literature on the writings of the local Russian diaspora, we

---

[1] Елачич, «письмо из Варшавы», Русская Книга (Берлин), 1921, № 5, стр. 17.

see a much larger influence occurring in Poland, despite mutual political issues.

2. The interwar Warsaw Russian diaspora and Filosofov

Warsaw had the largest Russian diaspora community in Poland and the diaspora's activities were supported by its own newspapers.

The Warsaw Speech (*Варшавская речь*) was first published in 1919 and was the first Russian-language newspaper published in independent Poland, highly praised Poland's independence based on historical legitimacy in its first issue. The impact of this newspaper was enormous, and almost all of the following publications of the Russian diaspora not only in Warsaw but also in other cities continued to support Poland.

This tone was consistent with Russian anti-Bolshevik expectations. During the outbreak of the Soviet-Polish War in February 1919, the Russian diaspora in Poland developed an anti-Bolshevik stance. In June 1920, *Svoboda* was first published in Warsaw. In 1921, *Za Svobodu* took over the newspaper. But the transition was merely superficial, as the editor did not change. *Za Svobodu* was published until 1932, followed by *Molva* (1932-34) and *Miecz* (1934-39). The four newspapers were all united in their anti-Bolshevistic endorsement of Poland's independence and, above all, in hopes that the relationship between Poland and Russia would improve.

On the other hand, one should remember that the exile newspapers, which had always been in opposition to Bolsheviks, would at the same time be a foothold for improving relations between Russia and Poland. The exile-poet Dmitry Filosofov (1872-1940) was involved in all of these newspapers and played a key role in Polish Russian diaspora activities for many years. He was one of the leaders of the late 19th century Russian art movement called the "Silver Age". After the Revolution and civil war he left Petersburg and came to Warsaw in 1920 via Minsk and Vilnius. Filosov developed a fierce anti-Bolshevist attitude and rejected both communism and imperial rule. While in Warsaw, he organized literary circles that worked in conjunction with the above-mentioned newspapers and helped support the development of exile culture, and to that end they were extremely significant.

Filosofov's literary circle in Warsaw was called "The Little House in Kolomna (Домик в Коломне)" after Pushkin's poem of the same title and it survived for two years (1934-36). It was modeled after Alfred Bem's "Tavern of Poets," which he had organized in Warsaw earlier. This circle was characterized by the participation of Russian as well as Polish writers and poets (such as Józef Czapski, Jerzy Stempowski, Maria Dąbrowska, and Julian Tuwim, or Marian Zdziechowski). The manifesto from the time of the group's formation is as follows:[2]

---

[2]In 1920, a group of Russian exile literary scholars, Tavern of Poets, was organized in Warsaw and worked together for nearly 25 years. The group was led by Alfred Bem, and among its participants were such figures as Boris Evreinov, and Vsevolod Baikin. Bem left the Warsaw in 1922, and headed over the new "Poets' Hermitage" in Prague, but continued close relations with Warsaw after his emigration. More than 150 poetry works created by "The Tavern of Poets" participants have been published in Polish Russian exile magazines and newspapers in Poland, especially in *Za svobodu!*. In 1923, they published *Six. A Small Almanac of Poetry and Prose* (Шестеро. Малый альманах поэзии и прозы). "The Tavern of Poets" also interacted with a Polish poets group "Skamander" (Julian

"As it is clear from the name, this is not intended to be a large group. The house is small and therefore is intimate. But Pushkin's name is linked to larger and broader themes. Pushkin has, in his creative personality, masterfully combined both that which is ethnic with the global. Therefore, by taking adopting Pushkin's name, this "Little House in Kolomna" also asserts itself worldwide as a tradition of Russian national literature."[3]

From the 1930s onward, the nationalistic and totalitarian trends in Soviet Russia gained more and more momentum. Filosofov, who was in the forefront of anti-Bolshevism, worried about this and created "The Little House in Kolomna" in hopes that it might improve bilateral relations of countries. To this end, the group was not a closed circle of only Russian exiles. Indeed, this "Little House" became a forum of exchange between the two countries' intellectual elites who lived in Warsaw.

Filosofov rejected those who did not conform to his political views, and because of this he had many enemies among the Russian exiles. However, as a symbolist poet, his goal was to restore the spirituality that he felt Europe was losing, and thus bring back harmony to mankind. He hoped to create a forum where Poles and Russians could integrate through art, sitting around a table with a Russian samovar (even though his was made of paper), that was a symbol of

---

Tuwim, Antoni Słonimski, Jarosław Iwaszkiewicz, Kazimierz Wierzyński and Jan Lechoń) formed in 1918. After the dissolution of "The Tavern of Poets", one of its most active participants, Vladimir Brand, joined the editors of *Molva* and later *Miecz* papers and published the poems of "The Tavern of Poets" members in these papers.
[3] Mitzner, Piotr. Warszawski „Domek w Kołomnie", Warszawa 2014, s. 7.

home.

3. Gomolicky as a Russian exile

One of "the Little House in Kolomna" participants, Leon Gomolicki (Lev Gomolitsky), was perhaps one of the most talented Russian-language poets of the interwar period in Poland. His personal history and the process of his creative activity are both very interesting. He began writing poetry in Russian as a boy, and after he appeared on the literary stage, he began to play a central role in the Russian diaspora in Poland. After the war, he used the Polish version of his name: Leon Gomolicki, and began to write exclusively in Polish.[4]

Lev was born in 1903 to a Polish family in Petersburg. His parents loved literature and he himself began to write poetry at the age of 12. His father was originally from Warsaw and worked as a military police officer when Lev was born. His parents met in the city of Penza, famous for its penal colony. Lev's maternal grandfather was a participant in the 1863 uprising.

He and his family moved from place to place in his childhood years. His father was a prison guard as part of his military police duties and lived away from home when Lev was a boy. Lev's father rejoined his family in autumn 1916, but for three years after this, the family continued to move from city to city in what now the border zone of western

---

[4] Refer to the following detailed description of the lifetime of Gomolicki. Лев Гомолицкий и русская литературная жизнь в межвоенной польше // Лев Гомолицкий. Сочинения русского периода / Под ред. Белошевской, Мицнера, Флейшмана. М. 2011. Т. 1. С. 5-282.

Ukraine. At the time of the 1917 revolution, Lev and his family lived in Łanowce (Lanovtsy). They then moved to Szumsk (Shumsk) and later to Ostróg (Ostroh), where they could settle down, at least for a moment in their restless life.

However, this quiet rural town which boasted, a history that went back to the Middle Ages, would not become their home. In autumn 1920, the Soviet-Polish War broke out and Lev's family headed for Warsaw, where Lev attended a Russian gymnasium (secondary school).

The family's stay in Warsaw coincided with the rise of publishing activities in Warsaw's Russian diaspora and this had a great impact on the poet's future. At that time, "the refugees" from Russia flowed into Warsaw in large numbers. It was around that time when Savinkov arrived in Warsaw and started the *Svoboda* newspaper together with Merezhkovsky and Gippius (June 1920). Despite the fact that he was still in his teene, Gomolicky had already begun to do creative work. Since he contributed to the newspaper, he became acquainted with Bem and Filosofov and through them was introduced to the Russian diaspora's literary circles. Initially, there were no literary columns in émigré newspapers, but a review of Alfred Bem's paper on Dostoevsky, published in February 1921, prompted them to establish space for literary articles. Eventually, newspapers began to publish Russian poetry, and Gomolicky's two pieces, 'Poet' and 'Children', were published on May 1, 1921and two more of his poems were published in September of the same year. However, due to Savinkov's deportation, *Za Svobodu* took over. In December of that year, Bem organized the literary circle "Tavern of Poets," but in January 1922, he left Warsaw and headed to Prague where he established a new literary circle called "The Hermitage".

After his deportation, a group of literary scholars who

were close to Savinkov published a poetry collection titled *Miniature* that consisted of pieces that had previously only appeared in newspapers. The volume was published during this period of confusion that surrounded Savinkov's deportation, quite an achievement in itself, and Filosofov greatly appreciated the collection. The question of what to publish next was, however, much harder to answer. In the midst of this Lev and his family left Warsaw and returned to Ostróg.

Piotr Mitzner has speculated about the reason why Gomolicky's family suddenly returned to Ostróg from Warsaw and points to the strong anti-Russian sentiment in the Polish capital shortly after the end of the war, which could have been unbearable for the family of a military police officer. On the other hand, for Russians, living in the Kresy territory would mean closer physical proximity to the "motherland". The ability to feel Russia's proximity, both geographical and cultural, while in a foreign land is something that the expatriates in Paris and Berlin could not experience. Ostróg, which was incorporated into the Soviet Union in World War II, was on the border between the two countries and it was a 'periphery' in two ways:it was away from both Russia and Warsaw- the capital city of émigré culture.[5]

In this periphery, the poet continued to create vigorously as anémigré. He learned about „The Poets' Hermitage" from the newspapers and wrote a letter to Bem and offered to participate. At the same time, Gomolitsky was active in the local cultural circle and published an anthology. He finally joined "The "Hermitage" in 1926 and was its only correspondent member. He sent many poems

---

[5] Там же. С. 12-13.

but was not highly regarded by other members. One of them remembered that "There is no modern feeling nor modern life (in Gomolicky's poetry)."[6] Eventually, Gomolicky left the frontier and went back to Warsaw in 1931 to take a new step.

4. "Warsaw" and Postwar Development

Leon Gomolicki recollected in his later years on how he decided to start in earnest as a literary writer:

"The story began in 1931 with a newspaper-led contest that triggered my debut in the literary circles. Unexpectedly, my short story won first prize, but the newspaper was suspended. *Molva*, which replaced it, was a more moderate newspaper, but it did publish my short story ('Night Encounter') in the first issue – a story about a foreigner who lives in the big city of Warsaw with no home nor job. One of the judges of this contest was Filosofov. […] When this newspaper was also suspended, Filosofov introduced me to *Miecz* and the literary salon "Little House in Kolomna." *Miecz* was supposed to be a bridge between Paris and Warsaw. Gippius was to be the editor-in-chief. The magazine looked like a brochure without a cover, and unfortunately, it was very short-lived. Paris took a condescending attitude toward us bumpkins, and was slow in responding to our requests, and on the other hand, for the Russian-language readers in Poland the magazine

---

[6] Вячеслав Лебедев, «Воспоминания о пражском "Ските"», «*Скит*». *Прага. 1922-1940. Антология. Биографии. Документы*, с. 715.

was too elitist. It was also Filosofov who put my poem "Warsaw" in the first issue."[7]

In the 1930s, Paris was home to the most prominent émigrés among the Russian diasporas around the world and the greatest cultural activities took place there. There was a clear gap between the communities, and the creative activities in Poland were far removed from those of Paris in terms of both quantity and quality. Nevertheless, for Gomolicky, who came to Warsaw holding fast to his ambitions, the "Little House in Kolomna," which was the center of Polish Russian diaspora, was certainly a big stage.

In 1934 he wrote a long poem titled "Warsaw" in Russian. In this highly autobiographical piece, which he dedicated to Filosofov, he depicted his starting point as a poet in childhood, his memories of poetry, and the loneliness of a young artist in Warsaw. The themes of "stranger" and "wandering" remained his favorite even after Gomolicky began to write prose in Polish. In "Warsaw", the bronze knight ran in Warsaw, not in Petersburg; the statue of Poniatowski rise, and the wind is compared to Chopin's curly hair. It depicts a Gomolicky's passion for poetry in a big city that is being cold to him.

"Warsaw" was a key turning point for Gomolicky, and the city of Warsaw was a special place for him. In 1945, he moved to Łódź, one of the largest cultural centersat that time, but he was very much eager to return to Warsaw.

In the end, however, Gomolicky did not return to Warsaw. After World War II, Lev Gomolicky adopted the Polish name Leon Gomolicki and composed all his poetry

[7] Леон Гомолицкий, «Воспоминания о Дмитрии Философове» (1981). Перевод Натальи Горбаневской. Новая Польша, 2006, № 9, с. 32.

not in Russian but in Polish. Furthermore, as a literary critic, he called himself a "critic-Russist (krytyk-rusycysta)" rather than a "Russian critic (krytyk rosyjski)", and as a literary scholar he specialized in Mickiewicz and Pushkin and published his works on the subject[8].

Gomolicki seems to have shed the persona of a "poet of the Russian diaspora in Poland". Perhaps one could argue that this was proof of his determination to live in the Polish society. In June 1945, after Poland had fallen under Soviet control, the poet joined the Polish Labor Party and the newly founded Polish-Soviet Friendship Society. His move to Łódź was a result of his appointment as the head of the Society's branch there. He also became a member of the Polish Writers' Union that year and a member of the Polish Artists Association in 1946.

Filosofov, who was his mentor in literature and had previously worked to build a bridge between Russia and Poland was one of the most eminent political figures in the Russian diaspora's literary circles. For him, a man at the forefront of the anti-Bolshevism movement, literature and politics were inextricably linked.

For Gomolicki, though, the problem of belonging was cultural, not political:

For us, the crucial life-and-death issue is not to bring the exiles together for any political goal or to decide about the League of Nations, nor has it anything to do with us working vigorously in Russia or with the fact that the Bolsheviks are growing in strength. Our future

---

[8] The following works deal with Pushkin and Mickiewicz: Leon Gomolicki, *Dziennik pobytu Adama Mickiewicza w Rosji 1824–1829*, Warszawa 1949, Leon Gomolicki, *Aleksander Puszkin*, Warszawa 1949; Leon Gomolicki, *Mickiewicz wśród Rosjan*, Warszawa 1950.

depends on there being some honorable people. At the very top there are those who inherit the great spirit of their nation: Lomonosov, Pushkin, Tolstoy, Andreev, Korolenko, Blok, and so many others – an amazingly long list. (Gomolicki, 'About the most important things')[9]

The existence of the first generation of exile literary scholars who left their homeland because of politics is in itself political. Their activities reached their peak in Russia prior to the revolution and, in most cases, when they later lived outside Russia, they would spend the rest of their lives anywhere in the world, with the mission of preserving that nostalgia and the Russian culture. On the other hand, the younger generations, who began their artistic activities or were born after the revolution and civil war lacked, from the beginning, a connection with the culture of the "motherland." Instead, these young generations had the opportunity to enjoy the cultural impact of the diaspora in a more direct manner. This is one reason why Gomolicki was able to "transfigure" from a Russian-language writer to a Polish-language writer with relative ease.

This also means that, as authors, the younger generations face fundamental problems. If the mission of an émigré writer is to protect their culture and traditions -that ia, to be in exile and try to earn a living by writing in Russian, how can they develop their art and style without assimilating his new environment? One could argue that is why younger generations generally tended to reject politics. The conflict of assimilation, perhaps a sense that this would

---

[9] Лев Гомолицкий, «О самом важном», Русский Голос, 1929, 21 июля, с. 2-3.

cause them to "abandon" the homeland, the desire to incorporate themselves into the genealogy of the homeland's culture, and consequently contribute to its "inheritance," has led to frictions between generations in the diaspora around the world. Assimilation, which in a sense no doubt means "abandoning" your homeland, or incorporating yourself into your homeland's lineage and, as a result, being able to contribute to its "heritage" – this dilemma has led to intergenerational conflicts in diasporas all around the world.

Concluding Remarks

In modern Poland, which has undergone repeated partitions and border movements over the years, people have equated the language, culture and art of the country with the vision of the country itself and have considered that they require the same protection. As a result, artists had to be more sensitive to identity issues. On the other hand, "place" is directly involved in the process of identity creation for any person. Among the poets who chose the path of assimilation one can see resignation, strategy and determination alike, and the experience of "place" by artists, including exiles, in Poland in the first half of the twentieth century is clearly tied to the artist's self-building.

7. Changes in National Identity over the Last 100 Years of Modern Polish Economy

Taku Okazaki
(Assistant Professor, Faculty of Management and
Administration, Tokiwa University)

Masahiro Taguchi
(Professor, Graduate School of Humanities and Social
Sciences, Okayama University / World Economy Research
Institute, SGH Warsaw School of Economics)

Introduction

In this paper, we would like to analyze "Polish identity" - the common theme of the International Scientific Conference on the 100th anniversary of Poland Regaining Independence from the economic perspective. The past 100 years of Polish economy can be analyzed in terms of national identity-building and transition. Building national identities means the establishment of economies that are not dependent on other countries and the creation of own social and economic systems rooted in their underlying traditions, cultures and geographic characteristics. This was an important process for the Polish people themselves to materialize independence and build stable political and economic relations with the neighboring countries.[1]

Modern Poland experienced three political and

---

[1] Chapter 1 and 2 were written by Taguchi, chapter 3 and 4 by Okazaki.

economic systems in just 100 years. These are: the establishment of the Second Republic following the regaining of independence in 1918, the establishment of a socialist political and economic system following the end of World War II in 1944, and the establishment of a capitalist system following the withdrawal from socialism and the systemic transformation in 1989. In this paper, we analyze the 100 years of Polish economy and describe what economic national identities have been found under each regime.

1. Restoration of independence and seeking for national identity

In the 20th century, Poland (the Second Republic) was freed from a long occupation of the Great Powers and became sovereign again. Poland was initially aiming to be a democratic republican nation. However, the emergence of economic statism (state interventionism) was permitted against the backdrop of inadequate infrastructure, economic vulnerability, discrepancies between foreign capital control and national interests, as well as the immature political systems.

Poland, which had recovered from a 123-year occupation of the Great Powers and had won independence, was a multi-ethnic nation with about 30% of ethnic minorities. According to the National Census in 1931, the country's population comprised of 68.9% Polish, 13.9% Ukrainians, and 8.6% Jews. Based on estimates by Jerzy Tomaszewski, taking into account differences in religion, the numbers can be readjusted to 64.7%, 16.0%, and 9.8%, respectively (Taguchi [2013], p. 20). This is a big difference from the current Polish state, where 95-97% of population is Polish. In principle, however, the various ethnic groups supported and developed the Polish economy under the occupation of the Great Powers. The question was how to integrate this into the national state community with common interests and mutual trust. At first, Piłsudski aimed to form a nation as a union of different ethnic groups. However, this philosophy eventually changed to an assimilation policy, although there were differences between regions. It is a fact that the problem of ethnic minorities was one of the major national challenges during the interwar period and that the rights of these minorities were not sufficiently protected. The new national identity was formed not as a multi-national but instead as that of a Polish nation-state.

Piłsudski was originally a military man and had no clear vision of economic policy. When the March Constitution was enacted in 1921, giving vast power to the Sejm (parliament), Piłsudski himself was drawn away from politics. However, after he gained power again in the May Coup (1926), he promoted state-led economic policies. In 1935, the amended April Constitution concentrated power in the president's hands. The newly independent Poland was originally oriented toward a freedom-based economy under a democratic republican system. It was not only a government policy, but also a course sought after by the economists and the business sector. From the beginnings of the Second Polish Republic, it was the trend of liberal economics influenced by the Cambridge School, the Neoclassical School, and the Austrian School that formed the mainstream of Polish economics. The Cracow School, led by Adam Krzyżanowski, showed the trends and the level of economics in Poland at the time. Krzyżanowski urged for restrictions of the economic activities of the state since its inception in the Second Republic. Krzyżanowski strongly opposed economic statism and cartels and called for economic liberalism based on private ownership. His idea was not limited to the field of economics. He thought that the disorder of parliamentary democracy was caused by the economic activities' deviation from the principle of democracy (liberalism), and from monopolies and state intervention becoming more prevalent. The business community was also originally strongly in favor of the liberal economy. Lewiatan, an association of private entrepreneurs, business persons and financiers, initially supported the Democratic Party (Endecja) and advocated maintaining a liberal market economy.

However, the economic foundation of Poland, which had just regained its independence, was fragile. It was essential for the state to take strong initiatives and introduce foreign capital. After the Great Depression and the withdrawal of foreign assets from Poland, the government was forced to take over the role previously played by the said foreign capital. As a result, many economists showed a certain level understanding towards the bureaucracy-led economic statism. The business community, in spite of its opposition to the economic statism, began to support Kwiatkowski, who promoted the construction of the Central Industrial Region (Centralny Okręg Przemysłowy: COP) after the Piłsudski's coup d'état.

Let us look at the details. In 1918, after the end of World War I, Poland was liberated from the Great Powers and regained its independence. However, the delay in modernization suffered under the Great Powers for more than a hundred years, as well as the human and economic losses caused by war were serious. 90% of the Polish lands were battlefields, with an estimated 400,000 dead and 800,000 injured. At the end of World War I, it is said that machinery and equipment in plants in the Warsaw Industrial Zone had receded to the level from the 1870s (Kaliński & Landau [1998], p. 40). Laws and business practices differed in the divided regions of Habsburg Austria, the Kingdom of Prussia, and the Russian Empire. Railways were also developed independently in the respective regions and were not connected at the borders. In addition, there was a large economic disparity between the western region (the so-called "Poland A") including Warsaw Prefecture and Kielce Prefecture, and the eastern region (known as "Poland B" or "Poland B, C") including Białystok, Lublin and Kraków Prefectures. Currently, this disparity affects not only the inequalities among local residents, but also the differences in their social ideas and voting behaviors. Given these initial conditions, it was natural that the government had to be deeply involved in post-war reconstruction and infrastructure development.

The new Polish Government took over the factories and production facilities left by the former governing countries after the end of their rule. These included railroads (excluding private railroads), forests, post offices, telegraph, distilleries (alcohol), salt refineries, tobacco production, gas pipelines, coal mines, steelworks, shipyards, banks, and printing companies.

Although Poland secured the access to the Baltic Sea under the Versailles Treaty in 1919, the city of Gdańsk in the estuary of the Vistula River became a Free City, which made it necessary for Poland to develop its own port and harbor as soon as possible. In September 1922, the construction of Gdynia Port began as a national project, with the government playing a leading role yet again.

In response to these national challenges, private firms did not have enough money to reconstruct factories and facilities destroyed in war. In addition, when the government was established, private enterprises were reluctant to make full-scale investments due to a fear of asset acquisition by the government. Therefore, the factors that promoted state market intervention in the immediate aftermath of World War I were the urgent need to establish the foundation for the establishment of economic activities as an independent state, and the prolongation of the war economy due to friction with neighboring countries after regaining independence.

During the interwar period, Poland was a typical agricultural country with an agricultural population of 69% or more (1931) and an industrial and handicraft population of 20% or less (1931). In addition to this backward trend, it was the stagnation of the economy that characterized the interwar period. Industrial production grew in the latter half of the 1920s when there was a global boom and in the latter half of the 1930s when state-led heavy industrialization was being pushed forward, but the industrial production generally saw little growth during the 20 years between the two wars.

Agriculture also slightly expanded in the latter half of the 1920s, but agricultural output at the end of the interwar period hardly changed from that at the beginning of the Second Republic. Moreover, the productivity was very low, and agricultural output per capita was less than half of that of Western Europe. Under such circumstances, the agricultural land reform was carried out (1921-1931), and a part of agricultural land owned by large landowners (about 10% of all agricultural land) was newly distributed to autonomous and tenant farmers. Nevertheless, as the land distribution was carried out, the new-born farmers were heavily in debt, and the condition of poor peasants hardly improved after all. At best, farmers purchased basic industrial products such as salt, matches, tobacco, saucepans, and some agricultural equipment but rarely spent money on sugar and clothing. Rural communities consumed only one-fifth to one-sixth of the supply of domestic industrial products.

Over the 20 years between the two wars, the underdevelopment of rural areas caused by the outdated agricultural structure and the stagnation of industries that could not find domestic markets due to rural poverty thus formed a vicious cycle. This stagnation created some serious social problems, such as large-scale unemployment in the cities and excessive rural population. It was especially in Poland that the aftereffects of the Great Depression prolonged, with an estimated 1,156,000 unemployed in 1935 and with unemployment rates reaching 39.9% (Landau &Tomaszewski [1999], p. 219). In addition, the labor force which was not absorbed by the cities stagnated in rural areas, resulting in overpopulation of rural areas (an estimated 2 million to 6 million people).

In 1926, when Piłsudski took control, the government became increasingly influential in the economy and society. However, after the coup d'état, Piłsudski did not adopt a superficial dictatorship system, and controlled the political conditions while preserving the functions of the Diet. As a result, political disruption was suppressed to some extent. The economy recovered in 1926-28, supported by the world's favorable trends, employment increased, and the currency stabilized. The fact of Polish state had securing control over the economic order was well received internationally and the reputation of Poland for foreign capital also increased. Taking advantage of these circumstances, the government actively sought to introduce foreign capital. In 1934, the share of foreign capital in Poland was 93.3% in the petroleum industry, 67.4% in the mining industry, 82.5% in the metal and refining industry, 70.1% in the chemical industry, and 82.4% in electricity, gas and water. Foreign capital become dominant in most of the key industries (Taguchi [2013], pp. 59-60).

In the latter half of the 1930s, economic statism rose noticeably in the government's economic programs. Foreign capital escaped from Poland due to the Great Depression, the rise of Hitler in Germany, and the increasing tension in political situation in Central Europe. As a result, it became necessary to rescue the industries abandoned by the foreign capital, and to strengthen national defense. Domestic capital, typified by Lewiatan, initially criticized economic statism. However, when it became clear that it achieved certain results in the economic recovery and that it would also bring benefit to the domestic capital, such statism met with more understanding. The new Constitution entered into force in April 1935, further strengthening the authority of the government. Since 1936, the Minister of Finance Kwiatkowski implemented a "Four-year Investment Plan" based on the expansion of public investment for industrialization. In 1937, the construction of a large Central Industrial Region (COP), accounting for one-sixth of the country's land, began. It was conceived as a "triangular zone" connecting Warsaw-Kraków-Lwów, which included 18% of the total population.

First, iron and metal refining complexes were built in Stalowa Wola, followed by weapon factories in Radom and Starachowice, production of light aircraft engines, machine tools and lighting equipment was set up in in Rzeszów, while chemical plants were built in Dębica. By September 1939, a budget of 400 million złoty and a workforce of 104,000 people had been invested. In addition, agricultural land reform was also carried out in parallel to ensure the labor force. In 1938, the "15-Year (Investment) Plan" was announced for enhancement of military potential, development of transport networks, promotion of agriculture as a support for industrialization, as well as promotion of industrialization and urbanization of towns and cities. In the latter half of the 1930s, the public sector accounted for 60% to 65% of Poland's total investment. In 1938, the share of state-owned assets in total national assets reached approximately 20%.

This government-led economic policy was not directed at developing fragile domestic capital or promoting SMEs. This policy focused on centralized resource allocation, in which the state became an investor to increase industrial capacity and prepare for possible international military conflicts. The government's attempts were, however, suspended by the outbreak of World War II. During the war, the German military used its production capacity for military purposes. Furthermore, in 1944, when the Soviet Red Army turned to counterattack, many of the factories were destroyed while others were disassembled by the German army and taken away to Germany, or similarly taken away by the Soviet Red Army later.

In the period between the two wars, parliamentary democracy and economic liberalism became the ideal principles and the economic reconstruction began. However, parliamentary democracy and economic liberalism were unable to support fragile economies. It can be said that the economic vulnerability of these emerging East and Central European nations was the background to the widespread support of the "small dictatorships" like Piłsudski's regime in Poland. That is, the national identity was built not in the direction of fostering private enterprises and creating a free and democratic state, but in the direction of creating a strong and stable Polish state that could compete against Germany and Russia at the expense of democracy.

2. Development strategy and its con-sequences in socialist Poland

The damage of World War II was enormous. Poland's financial losses amounted to about $50 billion, and the industrial capacity was reduced by about 50% due to destruction of factories and the removal of facilities abroad. Agriculture also devastated 20-40% of the total cultivated land area. The 6 million death toll meant that up to 22% of the population was lost. Such was the production and labor force handicap with which Poland had to begin its post-war reconstruction.

After World War II, the Polish border moved to the west in accordance with the Potsdam Agreement. As a result, Poland acquired Śląsk (Silesia) - a region rich in coal, tin, zinc and other resources, and favorable conditions for industrialization were created. In addition, the advanced agricultural methods and technology of the western recovered territories were expected to become instrumental in agricultural modernization. In the western recovered territories, the Germans who had lived there fled or were expelled, and as a result of the border change, many Polish peasants from Lithuania and White Russia, which were incorporated into the Soviet Union, settled in these lands.

In Poland right after the war, the construction of the

new system was defined by the agricultural land reform and nationalization of key industries. However, the non-socialized sector still accounted for a large portion of all the agricultural, industrial and commercial sectors. The concept of a mixed system based on the coexistence and equal development of the state-owned, cooperative, and private sectors was widely supported and later called a "three-sector system". It seemed to be an excellent solution to aim for an original way to socialism under the Provisional Government of National Unity, which encompassed both government members in exile and leftist forces.

However, as the East-West confrontation became more serious in 1947-48, the trend toward Stalinization intensified also in Poland. Against the background of this global situation, two important controversies were held. These are the "Battle for Trade (Bitwa o Handel)" (1947) and the "Debate on the Central Planning Office (Dyskusja CUP-owska)" (1948). In the "Trade Battle", restrictions on small private stores strengthened and the high-profit merchants were identified and taxed. On the other hand, the government took control of distribution and sales by semi-compulsorily organizing cooperatives and concentrating retail sales in state-owned department stores. In the "Debate on the Central Planning Office", intensive disputes arose over centralization of economic management and management system. Ultimately, in 1949, the Central Planning Office (CUP), which had gathered substantial power and inherited the traditions of economic policy from before World War II, was abolished. In place of the CUP a State Commission for Economic Planning (PKPG) was established to strengthen the national economic management.

The Six-Year Plan (1950-55), decreed in 1950,

accelerated the development of heavy industries linked to military industries under intense pressure of the Cold War , and led the economy on a path toward autarky. The plan was ambitious, setting a goal to increase industrial production by 158% over a six-year period. The Plan forecasted a 250% increase in investment compared to 1948, a 50% increase in agricultural production, and a 40% increase in the average real income of industrial workers. Based on this policy, the construction of hundreds of large-scale plants, including the FSO (Passenger Automobile Factory – started in 1948, opened in 1951) and the Nowa Huta Steelworks (started in 1949, opened in 1954), began one after another. Many of the plants relied on imports from the Soviet Union, and their payments were made primarily through low interest loans. The long-term trade agreement signed between Poland and the Soviet Union in June 1950 played a particularly important role in the industrialization of Poland. According to this agreement, Poland received a large supply of machinery and equipment. The industrialization process at that time was largely based on trade with and assistance from the Soviet Union. The outbreak of the Korean War in 1950 further accelerated the heavy industrialization route, centered on the munitions industry.

Agricultural collectivization also begun in earnest. In 1950, the State Agricultural Farms (PGR) were established by integrating various state-owned agricultural enterprises that existed by then. In rural areas, collectivization through organizing cooperative associations intensified. The names of farmers who did not participate in cooperative associations were posted in directly managed cooperative shops, which prohibited the sale of customer goods and farm equipment to them, and various forms of pressure were placed on the opposition groups.

Right after World War II, the aim was to establish a multidisciplinary political and economic system. However, as early as by the end of the 1940s, a dictatorial political and economic system was established. The Six-Year Plan, however, seems to had been initially successful within the rapidly unified system, but it quickly got stuck. In the first half of the 1950s, the development strategy, which prioritized growth in Department I (i.e. the production of means of production sector), was able to drive growth in heavy industries with extremely inclined investments, while causing the distortion of a chronic shortage of consumer goods. The underdevelopment of Department II (the production of consumer goods sector) resulted in lower standard of living for workers despite growth in gross domestic product. Agriculture was only able to achieve its planned production goal in the first year. Agricultural collectivization dramatically reduced motivation to produce, and individual farmers begun to refrain from investing in agriculture due to future insecurity. On the other hand, national financial support was focused on low-productivity state farms and not the private ones, which maintained relatively high productivity through self-help efforts even under such circumstances. The distortion was passed on to the people's lives in the form of a decline in workers' real wages and a decline in the supply of food and other consumer goods.

Khrushchev's "Secret Speech" criticizing Stalin at the 20th Congress of the Soviet Communist Party held in February 1956 impacted Poland. The upheaval of the socialist system that had seemed solid was apparent. In June of the same year, street protests that started with the issue of workers' wages at the multi-factory complex of Joseph Stalin Metal Industries (now the Cegielski Factory) evolved into riots. As a result, the army was dispatched and at least 75 people died in the events known as Poznań June (Poznański Czerwiec).

After the death of Stalin (1953), Eastern Europe entered the so-called "Thaw" era. Following the Poznań protests in 1956, the leadership of the Polish United Workers' Party (PZPR) was renewed, and Gomułka, who had been arrested, imprisoned in 1951 and criticized as a person with a "right-wing reactionary deviation", returned to the position of the First Secretary of the Party. He gained overwhelming public support by expanding consumer goods production, introducing a worker self-management system through the establishment of the Workers' Council, abandoning agricultural collectivization, reviewing economic relations with the Soviet Union, easing censorship and restoring relations with churches. In foreign relations, he exercised his skill in political and economic negotiations with the Soviet Union and West Germany. East-West relations were also gradually improved. In 1958, the COMECON restrictions (restrictions on exports to the Communist area) were relaxed, and the share of non-socialist countries in Polish foreign trade expanded to about 40%.

This way, the centralized economic system with the forced heavy industrialization and agricultural collectivization routes and the extremely Soviet-dependent external economic strategy failed in just a few years, forcing the national leadership to make a major revision. At that time, however, the leaders were focused on the development of key economic infrastructure and forming the foundation for the subsequent development of the Polish economy. Ironically, the pre-World War II concept of the construction of a Central Industrial Region was realized in a short time under the socialist system.

The Polish economic imbalance was corrected to some extent by the investment restraint policy starting in 1956, but the trade balance remained negative. One reason for this was that while the imports of fuels, raw materials, and materials increased, the exports were sluggish. Therefore, establishment of a raw material and energy supply base and strengthening of export output have become important medium and long-term issues. The "thaw" had fostered an international environment that expanded trade with capitalist countries. However, exports cannot grow without improvement in the quality of the exported goods exports. Therefore, modernization of the existing production facilities became an issue. In addition, plans were made for mechanization of coal mining and for development of sulfur mines to procure raw materials and fuels in Poland. In the long term, this was important for establishing a unique resource base. These plans, however, required huge investments and were not directly linked to final consumer product production. Despite these difficulties, Poland decided to expand its machinery exports in 1960 under the agreement with the COMECON countries, which created the possibility of economic modernization and export expansion. However, since the generation born in the post-war baby boom period had then reached the age of employment, and it was urgent to secure their workplaces. This became a prioritized issue and production modernization for the increase in labor productivity did not progress.

After all, collaboration and trade between Eastern European countries did not develop sufficiently. During this period Poland imported energy from the Soviet Union and imported modern machinery and equipment from the West, while exporting Polish machinery and chemicals to the Soviet Union, and agricultural products to the West to acquire foreign currencies. This kind of trade structure was completed under Gomułka's regime. This reality was far from the ideal COMECON cooperation and the establishment of an autarkic structure within the COMECON.

The failure of economic reforms and the slump in agricultural production in the latter half of the 1960s shifted the strain on consumer goods market. The government was forced to raise prices of meat and other food products. When it was announced in December 1970 that gross food prices would be raised, the anger among workers exploded violently. The outcry of those who felt that real wages were declining during the economic stagnation exceeded the government's expectations. The strike, which began at the Lenin Shipyard in Gdańsk, developed into a riot, shops in the city were attacked, and the local Polish United Workers' Party headquarters were set on fire by the demonstrators. The riots spread around cities along the Baltic coast, with approximately 100 companies in seven prefectures joining the strike. In response, the authorities were unable to suppress the situation by the police force alone, and finally dispatched the armed forces. The riot resulted in a total of 44 deaths and more than 1,000 injuries, and the Gomułka's regime was forced to resign ("December 1970").

The new regime, headed by Edward Gierek, greatly shifted its strategy from a closed self-sufficient economy within the CEMECON area to an open economy. Its Five-Year Plan (1971-75) aimed at achieving a national income growth rate of 38-39% over the five years, an industrial production growth rate of 48-50% and a real wage growth rate of 17-18%. Later, many of the basic indicators of the five-year plan were revised upward.

The new National Economic Development Strategy differed significantly from the previous strategy in that the Western loans provided both investments and increased consumption. Based on the new strategy, active licensing and plant introduction from the West were carried out with the aim of modernizing production facilities. Just as Brezhnev's regime was established in 1964 in the Soviet Union, the US - USSR détente was making progress, and Western financial institutions were looking for attractive investment destinations for stagflation money, so it was relatively easy to get loans from the West. This was in contrast to the views of Gomułka, who strongly detested borrowing from the West.

However, although the Polish economy initially appeared to be robust, various distortions began to emerge from around 1974. In the mid-1970s, the world's soaring prices for materials and energy caused by the oil shock led to a significant shortage of domestic supply of investment goods. Investment was tightened strictly since 1976, and the growth rate of investment, which was 10-25% in the first half of the 1970s, also slowed down to 1-3%. As a result, the growth rate of national income produced gradually declined to 3% in 1978.

Accumulated debt grew rapidly due to optimism based on the views that the debt could be repaid quickly if technology was introduced from the West, an inadequate outlook on the international perspectives, and a delay in responding to changes in the global market. In 1976, the trade deficit reached 9.7 billion transferable złoty. The cumulative debt to capitalist countries was about 3.9 billion transferable złoty in 1971, but increased to about 27.8 billion transferable złoty in 1975 and about 76.6 billion transferable złoty in 1980. In 1977, the total amount of medium- and short-term debt with high interest rates exceeded the total amount of long-term debt, which spurred an increase in interest rates on debt. In 1979, the growth was negative for the first time after World War II (-3.7%), and the National Income Produced decreased for the fourth consecutive year.

Even in the mid-1970s, when the long-term low-interest government loans were due, exports to the West did not expand as expected. Private banks' medium and short-term loans with high interest rates, which grew up due to loan refinancing, accounted for 26.8% of the total amount of loans in 1971, but in 1979 it was as much as 71.6%. Ultimately, short-term loans with high interest rates increased, resulting in a cumulative increase in interest rates.

On the other hand, in agriculture, production had been sluggish for a long time since 1974, and imports of grains, feedstuffs, meats and foods increased. Agriculture, which played a role in foreign hard currency procurement, became one of the factors contributing to the expansion of Western debt. Agricultural production growth declined significantly, from 1.6% in 1974 to -2.1% in 1975. In June 1976, the government announced a steep increase in food prices (meat/ham average 69%, sugar 100%, dairy products 50%, and vegetables 30%). After strikes and street demonstrations began in Radom and Ursus, the government had to give up price increases.

The economy worsened further without fundamental reforms. In July 1980, the Polish government once again announced an increase in meat prices. In response to this, strikes in numerous production plants began, with a call for the withdrawal of price hikes. The strikes spread nationwide again in a short time, and Gierek was forced to resign. The dissatisfaction among the people led to the establishment of the Independent Self-Governing Labor Union "Solidarity". Thus, Polish socialism's open economic policy was set back. Compared with the success of China's open economic policy, Poland was a loan-based, state-led investment in licensed production, which was undertaken by a government with little experience in investment risk. However, China developed a legal system and infrastructure environment for introducing foreign capital, and investment risk was undertaken by FDI foreign capital itself. This is a fundamental factor in the success and failure of both countries' economic policies.

The strikes, which began in July 1980, seemed to be settled in about a month, but in the middle of August the strikes spread again across the country. The strikes were led by a young electrician, Lech Wałęsa of the Lenin Shipyard in Gdańsk. The strike raised 21 demands (or "postulates"), including political calls such as free trade union approval, protection of strike rights, freedom of expression, and abolition of privileges for the members of the communist party apparatus. These actions quickly spread and echoed throughout the country.

After signing a political and labor agreement, the Independent Self-governing Labor Union "Solidarity" was successively formed among enterprises nationwide. Solidarity was the first autonomous labor organization under the socialist regime. Many workers withdrew from the former labor union led by the Polish United Workers' Party and participated in Solidarity. In rural areas, farmers' Solidarity groups were organized. Intellectuals and students also participated in the Solidarity movement which soon grew into a large social movement, far beyond the framework of labor unions, with 10 million people from the approximate total number of 21 million adults at the time). It is said that 1 million out of 3 million members of the Polish United Workers' Party participated in Solidarity.

However, with the expansion of the movement, the Party and the government perceived a crisis in upholding the regime and strengthened its stance against the Solidarity at the same time fearing the possibility of Soviet military intervention. Beginning in 1981, Solidarity gradually intensified and transformed from a self-limited movement, a social checking mechanism, to a movement aimed at overthrowing the government.

Under the Martial law, strengthening of censorship, prohibition of gatherings, advance notification of intercity travel, curfew, etc. were implemented. General Jaruzelski established the Military Council of National Salvation (Wojskowa Rada Ocalenia Narodowego: WRON) to strengthen military administration. This does not mean, however, that the economic reforms were back to square one. General Jaruzelski convened the Sejm (Diet) just after the introduction of the martial law, and vigorously implemented laws related to economic reform. As a result, legislation was developed to incorporate the reform proposals that had been required by Solidarity. General Jaruzelski's attitude towards economic reforms was somewhat similar to that of the reformists within the Party, thus the reformists were able to secure a certain level of influence. However, the fatigue of the socialist system was already so chronic that it could not have been healed by small-scale reforms.

Along with the sluggish shifts in politics and economy, the international environment was also changing little by little. In the Soviet Union, Gorbachev was appointed as the First Secretary of the Soviet Communist Party in 1985. In Poland, the 10th Meeting of the Polish United Workers'

Party was held in June 1986, and it was declared that the "normalization" (the process, which according to communist propaganda took place in Poland after the imposition of martial law) was "completed". In September of the same year, the government granted a pardon and released almost all political prisoners. This was the first step for the government to explore new ways of dialogue with the people in an attempt to "democratize" the system. In May 1988, the Soviet Union began withdrawing from Afghanistan. In July of the same year, Gorbachev visited Poland. Although he did not explicitly state the abandonment of Brezhnev Doctrine, this visit created an atmosphere of anticipation of change.

In August 1988, strikes started again in Lublin, Śląsk and Gdańsk. This was a wave of political strikes that clearly demanded the restoration of Solidarity. At this point, the Party was confident that it could not deal with the current situation in Poland without resolving political issues. In the same year, a meeting was held between Prime Minister Kiszczak and Wałęsa, who was in detention, and the strike was settled at the call of Wałęsa. At that meeting, an agreement was made to hold the Round Table Talks.

The general election was held in June based on the agreement reached at the Round Table Talks held from February to April 1989. The outcome of the partially free election was a Solidarity victory which exceeded expectations. Solidarity won almost all of the seats contested in a free vote. On the other hand, the Polish United Workers' Party was unable to acquire a single seat in the free election framework. Thus, after the general election, the Polish United Workers' Party has completely lost its resilience and lost its administrative power.

In the socialist period, Poland first aimed at building

its own economic system. However, the development of national identity was suppressed with the rise of the Cold War. After that, an attempt was made to build that identity within the frame of COMECON cooperation, but the establishment of a self-sufficient economic system led instead to stagnation. The 1970s' loan growth strategy achieved some success in modernization, but ultimately failed due to the cumulative debt crisis. National identities created under the special circumstances of the Cold War regime could not effectively form links with the global economy and did not promote innovation.

3. The Role of national growth strategies and the advancement of foreign multinational enterprises after the transition period

After the transition from the state-initiated market to the market economy, the main actors of the Polish economy shifted from the government and state-owned enterprises to the private ones, especially foreign multinational enterprises. In the share of newly sprung industries, the rise of Polish multinational enterprises came to the fore.

"The Round Table Talks" were held in February 1989, and a general election was conducted in the form of a partially free election in June. It resulted in a landslide victory for the "Solidarity" and the establishment of a non-Communist Party government. Along with the political change, the Polish economy also shifted from socialist to market economy.

Poland, however, faced a number of serious problems, including the deficiency of a price management system, large deficit in budget, soaring external debt, malfunctioning labor market (IMF [2014]). Under such unfavorable economic situation, the Balcerowicz Plan, formulated by the then Deputy Prime Minister and Minister of Finance, Leszek Balcerowicz, was formulated as a tool for Poland's transformation. The Plan was composed as a block of acts such as: measures for stabilizing the economy, system reforming, adapting social policy to the changes of the economic system, gaining foreign support for stabilization and system change programs. The Plan earned the nickname of "shock therapy" (terapia szokowa) because it focused on the short-term strategic stabilization through tightening credit. (Taguchi [2005]).

According to the plan for system change, one of the components of the block, a new market economy system was introduced, leading to the decisive shift of ownership from the state to private enterprises. With the advancement of privatization of former state-owned companies, foreign firms gradually came to enter into the market both through acquisitions (brownfield investments) and new investments (greenfield investments). This trend accelerated the improvement of Polish external economic relations compared with those during the socialist system period. Figure 1 shows the trends in the inflow of foreign direct investment (FDI) associated with such privatization processes. The FDI, which was very limited under the socialist economy regime, surged after the start of the regime change. This figure shows that the ratio of FDI to GDP also increased, and the presence of foreign firms in the Polish economy began to expand more markedly after the transition, continuing into the 1990s.

Figure 1 Foreign direct investment (FDI) inflow and FDI
to GDP ratio in Poland (1990-2017)

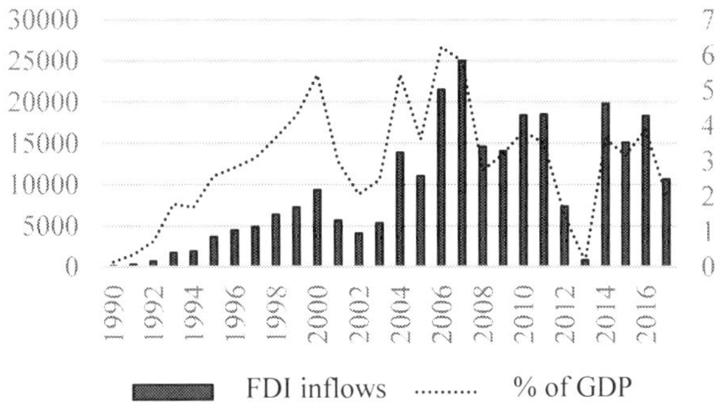

Left axis: FDI inflows (1 million US$); Right axis: % of GDP

Source: author's compilation from World Bank Open Data.

In conclusion, the 1990s, the transition period, was an age during which the main actors of the Polish economy transformed from state-owned enterprises to foreign multinational enterprises, and the foreign relations shifted from with the former COMECON to Western Europe and the U.S. and Asian countries including Japan and South Korea. In 1996, 66.1% of Polish exports and 63.5% of Polish imports were to and from the EU countries at the time, while trade with the former COMECON area was halved from around 40% to around 20% from 1989 to 1994 (Williams et al. [1998]).

In May 2004, Poland joined the EU along with other Central and Eastern European countries and became economically integrated into the single market of the EU. Since Poland became a member of the EU, continuous flow of investment has been kept except for a recession period prior to EU accession and during the post-European crisis period. In addition, the amount of trade with the EU, which was EUR 100 billion in 2005, nearly tripled to EUR 280 billion in 2017, and the relationship with the EU has greatly advanced from a standpoint of trade.

Poland has achieved stable economic growth compared to other Central and Eastern European countries since its transition to the new system and its accession to the EU. The Polish real GDP per capita, however, is only half of that of the EU, and the purchasing power at the 70% mark. These indexes show that Poland's economic level has not reached the average or higher level of the EU member countries. In addition, Polish economy, relying heavily on the EU funding and foreign firms, is fraught with grave problems such as uncertainties regarding the continuation of EU funding and the risk of being controlled by parent companies of the foreign firms in Poland.

Another issue is the delay in the Research & Development (R&D) sector of the economy. The ratio of R&D expenditure to GDP account for about 1% in Poland, which is about half the level of 2% in EU's 28 countries. Poland has not been expanding its high-value-added sectors nor relocating them from overseas, and the number of companies that have achieved innovation through R&D activities is still insufficient. The Polish government has also taken strong measures to address these problems since the 2010s. The National Research Programme was launched in 2011 as a roadmap for R&D sector development, and a "Strategy for Responsible Development" was announced in 2017. In this strategy, which aims at raising the standard of living of the people and achieving the average income level of the EU, corporate innovation development is placed high on the agenda. The Polish government seeks to change its policy from a growth path relying on the EU and other foreign countries' fund to the new policy aiming at fostering domestic economic growth factors (Taguchi [2017]).

On the other hand, the business services sector, including IT outsourcing, has been growing in recent years. Domestic employment in this sector also increased by 30%, from 214,000 in 2016 to 279,000 in 2018 - an annual growth by 14% (ABSL [2018], p. 9). As a novel tendency, some developing Polish firms have emerged in the new industries such as IT outsourcing service and are trying to acquire German firms. Under the ongoing foreign dependent economy, these newly emerged and global-oriented enterprises, trying to develop far and wide in the world, occupy only a small proportion of Polish firms, but the trend shows unprecedented inclination.

After the political transition, foreign firms began to enter into the Polish market economy, and overseas capital started to flow, which led to the formation of the new Polish economic and industrial identity. The fact that foreign capital and firms play decisive roles contributes greatly to the establishment of the new identity. Since its accession to the EU, Poland's integration into the EU economy and integration into the global production network have progressed, with the emergence of domestic global and tackling the burning issue of launching into the advanced sectors of industry. Under these circumstances, a novel economic identity began to take shape. The newly formed identity is centered on a "New Polish Economy", the purpose of which is to grow out of from the old-fashioned low-waged, low value-added production and produce high-value-added products and services.

4. Changing identity in the case of the Polish automotive industry

In this chapter, we will take a look at the automobile industry, which is one of Polish core industries with long tradition and examine the progress of the transition of the economic identity at the industrial level in concrete terms.

The Polish automobile industry had a long history beginning in the interwar period and had strong ties with the national policy. In the times when various kinds of industries sprang up, car industry strengthened the link with domestic security policy by producing military vehicles. Under the socialist regime, two state-owned companies, Fabryka Samochodów Osobowych (FSO) and Fabryka Samochodów Małolitrażowych (FSM), became the core companies of passenger car manufacturing. After the change of regime, FSM was acquired by FIAT, which had previously been affiliated with FSM, and the commercial/agricultural vehicle manufacturer FSR (Fabryka Samochodów Rolniczych) was acquired by Volkswagen (hereinafter referred to as VW). FSO, a major state-owned manufacturer, was acquired by the South Korean Daewoo. Unfortunately, Daewoo's parent company, collapsed not long after, leaving FSO forced to seek a new buyer. Ukrainian companies did acquire it, but production has been suspended.

During the transition period, the former state-owned automobile companies were sold out, which resulted in the entry of major overseas manufactures through acquisitions (brownfield investment). FIAT, who took over FSMs, played a leading role in producing passenger cars. The supplier structure was also formed by the Italian suppliers' entry into the Polish market, and the role of foreign companies in Poland expanded.

From the late 1990s to the 2000s, when Poland groped its way toward joining the EU, new investments (greenfield investment) were also seen in the automotive industry. In 1996, Opel entered the Polish market to produce finished vehicles. Toyota also established TMMP in 1999 and TMIP in 2002, beginning to produce engines and transmissions. The expansion of these foreign manufacturers was accelerated through greenfield investments without acquisitions, and further advanced the clustering of automotive production areas in southwestern Poland. These areas had developed in terms of industry and economy by producing vehicles for FIAT.

Foreign makers including Toyota and VW have promoted production of engines and other parts in Poland. The automobile parts produced in Poland were supplied to Central European countries such as the Czech Republic and Slovakia, and to Western Europe. These trends have led Polish car industry to being incorporated into the European automotive production networks as a major player in supplying car parts. The new trend in the automobile industry indicates the shift in the production mode from the passenger car production by state-owned manufacturers to the production by multinational manufacturers besides the market shift to the EU market.

In recent years, new forms of development have been initiated in the automobile industry. This is because car makers are forced to tackle the global changes caused by environmental regulations and the requirement for producing electric-powered vehicles. The Polish automotive industry has also been following the worldwide current of the times. One of the countermeasures against the hindrances stemming from environmental protection is to develop the R&D sector. Car makers such as Delphi, WABCO and Faurecia have founded R&D divisions and facilities, and the Polish car producers, led by foreign makers, have also made some progress in the R&D sector.

In addition, measures have been taken in the sphere of producing low-emission and environment-friendly vehicles including EVs and other next-generation automobiles. In Poland, trends toward battery production for EVs and other next-generation automobiles have been confirmed. In addition, Solaris, a domestic commercial car manufacturer has been accelerating the production of electric buses to cope with the industrial evolution.

As described above, major multinational manufacturers entered Poland through acquiring the former state-owned enterprises and making greenfield investments after Poland became a member of the EU. As a result, the Polish industrial structure changed from production by state-owned manufacturers in the socialism economic system to production by foreign multinational manufacturers. Polish industry has been incorporated into European production networks as a manufacturer of vehicles and supplier of parts, especially engines. Thus, the automotive industry clearly and graphically demonstrates the characteristics of the Polish industry – changing the key players of the industry during the period of the transition of the regime and the accession to the EU. The shift of major players was the primary cause of the identity change in economy. The traditional identity formed by the state economic system operated by the state-owned enterprises has shifted to new identities created through close collaboration with EU and foreign multinational corporations.

Concluding Remarks

In Poland during the Second Republic Period (the interwar period), while there were attempts to build a new nation based on economic liberalism and parliamentary democracy, it was difficult to build a strong nation without state-led industry development and the introduction of foreign capital. As a result, Piłsudski's coup d'état was also widely supported as a way establishing a strong and stable regime. After the Great Depression, the government led the construction of the Central Industrial Region and promoted the development of key industries. This became a symbolic undertaking in the process of economic national identity building. However, the construction of the Central Industrial Region was abandoned in World War II.

After World War II, the government initially aimed at building People's Democracy based on pluralism. However, as the Cold War intensified, rapid heavy industrialization and forced agricultural collectivization were introduced. Stalinist economic development strategy has gotten stuck in just a few years, but since the end of the 1950s, industrialization was carried out again, concentrating in the resource development and machinery and chemical industries development based on the international division of industry within the COMECON. Industrialization with the emphasis on capital goods production had negative impact on the consumer needs of the people but in the long term, it cannot be denied that the industrialization constructed the broad basis of the Polish economy (see: Piatkowski [2019]). The economic openness since 1970 was aimed at modernization through the introduction of licenses from the West, but new investments did not promote exports and the cumulative international debts increased. In the wake of the economic crisis, the "Solidarity" protest expanded to the national movement, but it did not lead to a fundamental change in the economic system. Economic reforms were also attempted in the 1980s, but socialist economic system itself was unable to adapt to the global economic trends since the 1980s driven by innovation and lost their growth potential.

Growth during the transition period was driven by radical liberalization policies that drastically improved economic imbalances. As a result of the expansion of foreign capital into Poland, including the automobile industry which has a particularly broad base, orders received by domestic intermediate goods manufacturers have increased, and technological bottoming out by foreign capital guidance has rapidly progressed. Improvements in export output have also been remarkable due to growth in production by foreign-affiliated companies. In contrast to the Second Republic period, foreign capital played a major role in the development of domestic industries. By the end of the 1990s, the business conditions of Russian economy had hardly affected Polish economy, and the EU shift in industries was rapidly advanced during the transition period. The acceptance of the *Acquis Communautaire* and the accession to the EU have become the basis for Poland to share identity with the EU. In addition, the impact of the global financial crisis in 2007 was minimal because the manufacturing sector was the basis for growth, and Poland maintained positive growth in 2008, even when most European countries fell to negative growth.

In this paper, we have examined the change during the transition period, taking the automobile industry as an example, and it can be said that the Polish automobile industry has shifted from the economic national identity based on state-owned enterprises and national strategies to the identity based on the linkage between foreign multinational enterprises and the EU economy through the change of major actors in the industry. As a result, although Poland has been pursuing economic growth in partnership with foreign capital, it has not been able to form a sustainable and autonomous economic national identity because of the deep-rooted nature of the subcontracting of foreign multinational enterprises. Polish government should adopt an economic policy that establishes an innovation-promoting industrial structure and develops distinctive and competitive industries while the inflow of foreign capital and steady growth continues.

References

[Japanese literature]
Hiroichi Iemoto (2015). 'Why does Poland continue to grow positively?', Institute of Eurasian Studies [http://yuken-jp.com/report/2015/09/15/poland/] (Access: 2019.04.20).
JETRO [2001]. 'Current Status of Privatization Aiming at Enhancing Economic Efficiency and Competitiveness (Poland)', *Euro Trend*, No. 47, pp. 143-171.
Masahiro Taguchi [2005]. *Political Economy of the Collapse and Generation of the Polish Transformation System*, Tokyo: Ochanomizu Shobo.
Masahiro Taguchi [2013]. *Economic Development of Modern Poland. Political Economy of Growth and Crisis*. (Economic Studies Research Series of the Faculty of Economics, Okayama University, No.42), Faculty of Economics, Okayama University.

Masahiro Taguchi [2017]. 'Poland's Strategy for Responsible Development', Institute of Eurasian Studies [http://yuken-jp.com/report/2017/08/06/polska/] (accessed May 2, 2019)

Mitsuyoshi Matsuura [2016]. 'Polish Economy and Middle Income Trap', *Russia and Eastern Europe Studies*, No.45, pp. 170-183.

[Foreign Language Literature]

ABSL [2018] *Business Service Sector in Poland 2018.*

Electrive.com 'Solaris Ramping Up Electric Bus Market Share' [https://www.electrive.com/2019/03/09/solaris-strategy-aligns-for-ramping-up-market-share/] (Access: 2019.05.10).

GUS [2018a] *Handel zagraniczny Polska w Unii Europejskiej; Foreign trade. Poland in European Union.*

GUS [2018b] *Rocznik Statystyczny Handlu Zagranicznego. Yearbook Trade of Foreign Statistics of Poland.*

Haanes, Knut, Harald Hvidsten and Peter Lorange [1997] 'The Transformation of Fiat Auto Poland', Thomas, Howard, Don O'Neal and Raúl Alvarado Sibaja (eds.) *Strategic Discovery: Competing in New Arenas.* New York: Wiley, pp.315-333.

Havas, Attila [1997] 'Foreign direct investment and intra-industry trade: the case of the automotive industry in Central Europe'. *The technology of Transition: Science and Technology Policies for Transition Countries*, pp.211-240.

IMF [2014] '25 Years of Transition Post-Communist Europe and the IMF'.

Jarosz-Nojszewska, Anna (ed.) [2017] *Problemy*

gospodarcze Trzeciej Rzeczypospolitej. Warszawa: Oficyna Wadawnicza SGH.

Kaliński, Janusz, Zbigniew Landau [1998] *Gospodarka Polski XIX i XX wieku.* Warszawa: PWE.

Kaliński, Janusz, Czesław Noniewicz [2015] *Historia gospodarka Polski w XX wieku.* Białystok: Wyd. Uniw.w Białymstoku.

Landau, Zbigniew, Jerzy Tomaszewski [1999] *Zarys historii gospodarczej Polski 1918-1939.* Warszawa: KiW.

Piatkowski, Marcin [2014] 'The Warsaw Consensus: The New European Growth Model', in: Kolodko, Grzegorz (ed.) *Management and Economic Policy for Development*, New York: Nova Science Publishers, pp.309-332.

Piatkowski, Marcin [2019] *Europe's Growth Champion: Insights from the Economic Rise of Poland*, Oxford: Oxford UP.

Williams, Allan M., Vladimir Balaz and Stefan Zając [1998] 'The EU and Central Europe: The Remaking of Economic Relationships', *Tijdschrift voor Economische en Sociale Geografie,* Vol.89, No.2, pp.131 – 149.

World Bank Open Data [https://data.worldbank.org/] (Access: 2019.04.25).

8. Polish identities in Prussian Poland

Satoshi Warita

(Professor, Aoyama Gakuin University)

Introduction

The term "Prussian Poland" refers to the four eastern provinces of Prussian-Germany: Posen, East Prussia (Ostpreussen), West Prussia (Westpreussen), and Silesia (Schlesien). These provinces outlined the eastern border region of the German Empire and had a mixed German and Polish population.

This paper focuses on the province of Posen. While relationships between Polish and German people varied from region to region, Posen has been described as a typical example of the ethnic conflict between Polish and German people.

In recent years, historical science has gained a common understanding that, in the modern period, both nations and national identities are formed together. Since there was no Polish nation-state in the 19th century, the consciousness of a "Polish" identity should be regarded as being formed in the modern era. Various versions of sense of nationality, however, were formed in partitioned Poland, along with the term "Polish."

For example, the German historian Hans Schmitt, in his 1912 work, referred to a newspaper article from 1858, noted:

In the Grand Duchy of Posen, the position of the Polish resident, if one considers him as a man and a citizen, is freer and safer than in Galicia and in the Kingdom, but if one considers him as a Pole, it is the most difficult and unbearable. (Schmidt 1912, p.77)

In each area of partitioned Poland, Polish people lived under different conditions. In Posen, life as a "Pole" was particularly difficult. From this, it can be inferred that Polish people who had been recognized as a national group by others formed their own consciousness in the partitioned territories.

As another example, British historian Lewis Namier touched on the Slav Congress in his work "*1848: the revolution of the intellectuals*":

At one meeting at which no Pole was present, Brauner told an anecdote of how peasants in the district of Sącz in West Galicia, when asked whether they were Poles, replied: 'We are quiet folk.' 'Then are you Germans?' 'We are decent folk.'. (Namier 1946, p.107, note 2)

Sącz was a city in the former Kingdom of Poland. However, this statement showed that the peasants in the Sącz region did not recognize themselves as either Poles or Germans. In other words, there was a difference in consciousness among social groups, and the peasants did not have, or did not care about having, a national identity, whereas the upper and middle classes were considered Polish.

These descriptions indicate that the sense of nationality

of Poles differed within (1) areas of partitioned Poland, and furthermore, within each region and (2) social stratum, class, or group. In other words, the sense of nationality of Poles was diverse, and there was no single national identity.

In the province of Posen, the pressure of the Prussian-German government on Polish society would increase the sense of nationality of the Poles and spread to a broader section of societies. We consider the characteristics of the formation of the "Polish" consciousness in the province of Posen in the following sections.

1. Prussian Poland

At first, we must define the region which we call Prussian Poland. Prussian Poland consisted mainly of the four eastern provinces of the German Empire. We will discuss each region in the order of territorial occupation by the Hohenzollern family.

The Hohenzollern family took control of East Prussia in 1618. After gaining independence from Poland in 1660, the Hohenzollern family won the Prussian throne in 1701, based on their foothold in East Prussia. Next, the family took control of the province of Silesia after the Austrian Succession War (1740-1748) and the Seven Years' War (1756-1763). In 1772, the province of West Prussia was incorporated by the first partition of Poland in 1772. It merged with East Prussia in 1824 and was known as the Province of Prussia until 1878. By the second partition of Poland in 1793, the Posen region known as Wielkopolska (Greater Poland) had become a Prussian territory. Wielkopolska region became part of the Duchy of Warsaw in 1807 during the Napoleonic Wars but was returned to

Prussian control in 1815 after the Congress of Vienna and formed the province of Posen.

Each province had a different historical background based on its time within the Kingdom of Poland. The provinces were further affected by the time period wherein they were acquired or annexed by the Hohenzollern family. Therefore, the area should not be recognized as a single, integral region.

However, the establishment of Germany by the Kingdom of Prussia in 1871 led to the incorporation of Prussian territories into the German Empire. After that, the four eastern provinces became recognized as "Prussian Poland" because of their common characteristics: the provinces were in the eastern section of Prussia and the German Empire and contained relatively high concentrations of Polish people.[1]

Posen was consistently characterized by its higher proportion of Poles compared to German families throughout the 19th century. From 1861 to 1890, the population of Germans increased from 679,584 to 697,286, while that of Poles increased from 805,366 to 1,053,877 in the province of Posen. The Polish population was not only higher than the German population, but the rate of increase was also higher. This discrepancy affected the policies of the Prussian government on Posen.[2]

2. "Language, Religion, Nationality" as Privileges

The province of Posen was incorporated into Prussia in

---

[1] Kopp 2012, p.22.
[2] Böckh 1894, pp.428-430.

1815 after the Congress of Vienna with the "Patent wegen der Besitznahme des Preußen zurückfallenden Theiles des Herzogthums Warschau (Patent for the possession of the parts of the Duchy of Warsaw which are returned to Prussia)" and the proclamation "An die Einwohner die Großherzogthums Posen (To the inhabitants of the Grand Duchy of Posen)": [3]

As by my todays' act (*Patent*) of [territorial] possession I have brought back to its ancient conditions that part of the former Warsaw Duchy counties which had originally belonged to Prussia and have now been returned to My Country, I was prudent to stipulate your conditions as well. You too have a Fatherland (*Vaterland*) and along with it you have likewise received a proof of my regard for your attachment to it. You will be incorporated into My Monarchy, without letting your nationality (*Nationalität*) to be lost. You will participate in the Constitution that I intend to grant to my faithful subjects and you will get a provincial system (*eine provinzielle Verfassung*) like the rest of the provinces of My Kingdom (*Reich*).

Your religion shall be maintained (...). Your personal rights and your property return under the protection of the laws, which you should consult for advice in the future.

Your language shall be used in addition to German in all public proceedings, and everyone among you should, according to his abilities, have access to the public offices of the Grand Duchy, as well as to all

---

[3] *GS* 1815 pp.45-47.

offices, honors and dignities of My Kingdom (*Reich*).[4]

This document showed what the King of Prussia guaranteed to the province of Posen: language, religion, and nationality. Both German and Polish were to be recognized as provincial languages and both the Protestant and the Catholic religions were to be recognized in the province, defined as "You" in the proclamation.

Interpreting what was meant by nationality, however, was more difficult. Considering the context of the paragraph, nationality can be interpreted as a political right rather than cultural or national characteristics which make up an ethnicity. Simultaneously, considering that the act guaranteed personal rights and property, the "inhabitants" should be regarded as the upper levels of society who owned a certain amount of property, not as inhabitants at all levels of the society. We should consider that a certain level of political independence was guaranteed only to the upper levels of society in this patent.

The document has often been interpreted as an acknowledgment of only Polish rights. However, since the provincial assembly of the Posen was first held in 1827, its members were elected based on land ownership; in order to having political rights, property was needed. The act also demanded that the two languages be treated equally.

The act of 1815 recognized the three elements of language, religion, and nationality for the province of Posen. As a result, it can be said that the languages (Polish and German), religions (Catholic and Protestant), and political independence of the upper levels of society were approved as the rights of the province. These three elements should be

---

[4] *GS* 1815 p.47.

considered societal privilege in the first half of the 19th century.

In 1832, the Oberpräsident of the province of Posen issued a Language Ordinance which ordered that German be adopted as the administrative language of the province. However, this did not cause major disturbances in practice; the use of both languages was maintained.[5]

On March 20, 1848, an uprising in the province of Posen led to the beginning of a revolution. Polish activists demanded the autonomy of the province of Posen. This uprising was a response to the demand throughout most of Germany for the establishment of a unified German state. Polish activists in Posen rose up and refused to be incorporated into Germany. At the end of April, the Polish armed forces and the Prussian military clashed, and the Polish army was defeated in May. The uprising was not universal; the Polish armed forces included only a few thousand people out of about 680,000 Polish speakers in Posen.[6]

The 1848 revolution in Germany and the campaign to create a unified Germany led to the Frankfurt National Assembly and the development of the German Constitution. The Frankfurt National Assembly also wanted to incorporate Posen and West Prussia into Germany, but due to the fighting in Posen, proposed to divide the province into German and Polish sections, which led to a debate over the border. The Frankfurt National Assembly ultimately failed

---

[5] *AP* 1832, No.22 (29 Mai 1832), pp.195-198; *AB* 1832, No.23 (8 Juni 1832), pp.453-457.
[6] This number was an estimate. See, Bergmann 1883, p.31. Bergmann showed the following numbers on the inhabitants in Posen in 1846: German speaker 380,085, German and Polish 281,444, Polish 681,531.

in creating a unified German state, however, and Posen was not separated into new partitions.

While it is accurate to say that the Polish in Posen had consistently rejected incorporation of Posen into Germany, we should consider that the broader group of Poles as a whole did not resist, even during events that were considered important for Polish identity, such as the language decree and the Posen uprising of 1848. This suggests that in the first half of the 19th century the notion of Polish national consciousness was limited to some upper social groups.

3. Popularization of Polish consciousness

In Posen, Polish consciousness spread to the wider public after the establishment of the German Empire during 1871 into the early 20th century.

When the German Empire was established in 1871, the province of Posen became one of its parts. Otto von Bismarck, the Minister President of Prussia and the Chancellor of the German Empire, adopted a policy called "negative integration" for national integration of the German Empire. This was aimed at integrating the majority by creating and suppressing the *Reichsfeinde* (enemies of the Empire). These enemies included political Catholicism, parliamentary liberalism, social democracy, liberal Jews, and national minorities.[7]

Catholics predominantly lived in the newly incorporated South Germany. The Roman Catholic Church was incompatible with the German nation state because it

---

[7] Wehler 1973, pp.96-100.

recognized the supreme papal authority in matters of faith and discipline. As a result, they were labelled as enemies of the empire. The conflict between the German imperial government and the Roman Catholic Church was called *Kulturkampf* (cultural struggle). National minorities included non-German peoples within the German Empire, such as Poles, Danes, and the people of Alsace-Lorraine. Since many Poles were also Catholic, they were doubly enemies of the empire. On the other hand, a "standard German" was the exact opposite of an enemy of an empire; they were of German descent, spoke German, and were Protestant.

The Prussian-German government implemented a series of repressive policies against Polish society called *Polenpolitik* (Polish Policy). *Polenpolitik* were mainly implemented in three areas: the Catholic Church, land struggles and language.

(1) Laws Opposing the Catholic Church

During the *Kulturkampf* period of the 1870s, provisions were enacted that directly opposed the Catholic Church. The School Inspection Law of March 1872 regulated that all school inspectors were officials of State. This meant that clergymen no longer had the authority to supervise school education.[8] In addition, the May Laws of 1873 were aimed at creating state control over the priesthood, eliminating church disciplinary rights, and restricting the Church's jurisdiction.[9] The *Kulturkampf* gradually decreased its intensity to gain support of Catholics for other government proposals, such as the Anti-Socialist Laws in 1878.

---

[8] *GS* 1872, p.183.
[9] *GS* 1873, pp.191-208

The laws to weaken the authority of the Catholic Church served as repression against Polish people in the eastern provinces as many of them were Catholics. Even after the government settled with the Catholic Church in the 1880s, the struggle continued in practice within the province of Posen.

(2) Conflicts Over Land Rights

Land conflict was the most straightforward means of oppression; the land was taken from its Polish owners and attempts were made to settle Germans there. *Ansiedlungsgesetz*, the law concerning the promotion of German settlement in the provinces of West Prussia and Posen, was enacted in 1886. The law invested 100 million marks to purchase the land of Polish aristocrats in order to strengthen the "German element (Deusches Element)" in the two provinces.[10] However, this did not produce the desired results. Polish landowners countered this policy by establishing the Land Bank, which financed estate maintenance.[11]

In order to leverage this policy, additional funds were invested. Furthermore, the New Colonial Law was passed in 1904[12] and the Land Expropriation Law was enacted in 1908[13], but since only four Polish estates were acquired at above market prices with 1650ha, the expected effects were not achieved.[14]

(3) Language Policies

---

[10] *GS* 1886, pp.131-134.
[11] Blanke 1981, pp.94-97.
[12] *GS* 1904, pp.227-234.
[13] *Preußische Gesetzsammulung*, 1908, Nr.7, pp.29-34.
[14] Perdelwitz 1936, p.94, Blanke 1981, p.232.

The most serious issue for the national consciousness of Polish people was how their language was associated with the cultural and inner lives of individuals. Policies regarding the status of Polish and German languages were put in place. Although issues arose in various environments, they were particularly notable in government offices and schools.

Polenpolitik laws relating to the Polish language began with the founding of the German empire. On October 16, 1872, Prussian Minister of Education issued a regulation ordering that the religious classes at senior schools in Posen should be taught in German. On October 27, 1873, the Oberpräsident of Posen issued orders making German the chief language of instruction in all elementary schools and giving Polish only an auxiliary role and only when necessary. Only religious classes and religious songs were taught in Polish, and then only for children in lower grades. In middle and upper grades, these classes were also conducted in German, if the children spoke the language well. Polish was only accepted when it was taught as the subject of the class.[15]

In 1876, the Prussian government enacted the Official Language Law. This law made German the only official language in administration and all public institutions. There was a transitional period where Polish was phased out, but this eliminated the administration's bilingual system in Polish regions. As a result, Polish-only speakers were effectively forced into the position of second-class citizens. However, the Polish language was accepted in public and private lives that were not related to the state.[16]

Since the formation of the German Empire, the

---

[15] Korth 1963, pp.40-42.
[16] *GS* 1875, pp.393-394.

repression of Polish language had been consistent. The Polish people, however, did not fight back, even when the official language law was enacted. The struggles between Polish and German status reached their peak in the schools at the at the beginning of the 20th century.

In 1900, the Prussian government prohibited private Polish reading and writing lessons outside the formal school curriculum. In addition, at elementary schools (*Volksschule*), religion classes for middle and upper grades were to be taught in German; Polish language classes as a subject were abolished. By intervening in religious teaching, the state was involving itself in the formation of individuals' inner lives.

On May 20, 1901, at an elementary school in city of Września (Wreschen), students who refused to recite the teacher's words or read a biblical text in German were punished by the teacher. This event triggered the Września affair, a series of strikes at regional schools.[17]

School strikes became more common until they reached their peak in 1906. At the time of Easter in 1906, 203 more schools were forced to introduce religion classes conducted in German. On October 14, 1906, Stablewski, archbishop of Poznań and Gniezno, issued a pastoral letter appealing for the importance of religious lessons in their mother tongue to be recognized. This letter became a motivation for the general school strike in Prussian Poland; the school strikes occurred mainly in the provinces of Posen and East Prussia. Strikes continued for almost another year, into 1907. There were various forms of strikes as passive resistance: pupils, following their parents' instructions, refused to answer questions in religious class, to sing hymns, or to pray in

---

[17] Korth 1963, pp.89-92.

German. People also protested in front of the schools. Pupils, parents, schools that participated varied day by day; a total of over 1,600 schools with 93,000 children participated in the school strikes.[18]

This was a significant number of participants for the time. There were 240,808 Polish-speaking school children in Posen in 1906[19], which means that nearly 40 percent of the students in the region were participating in school strikes. Those Poles who had not been pushed towards a revolt when the government interfered with the public life expressed great opposition when the government interfered with religion and with the language in which that religion was taught. This was because government policy had conflicted with the inner life of individuals. From the perspective of Poles, this pushed them towards a national identity as Polish people. The spread of school strikes indicated that the consciousness of Polish speaking Poles as separate from German speaking Germans was beginning to spread to the broader public.

In Prussian Poland, particularly in the province of Posen, the consciousness of a Polish identity had spread to the public in the early 20th century. The main cause of the popularization of Polish consciousness in the province of Posen was the *Polenpolitik* created by the Prussian-German government and the Polish reaction against it.

These circumstances gave rise to a Polish consciousness that was different from those created in Russian and Austrian territories. In addition, the consciousness of the Polish people of Prussian Poland also varied from region to region; because of this, the shape of

---

[18] Kulczycki 1981, pp.111-112.
[19] *Preussische Statistik*, Bd.209. Heft.3 (1908), p.334.

the Polish identities discussed here are primarily characteristic of the province of Posen.

Concluding Remarks

We have investigated the formation of Polish consciousness in the province of Posen. The characteristics of Polish consciousness in Posen could be ascribed to the *Polenpolitik* of the Prussian-German government against Polish speakers and to the formation of the collective awareness of Polish speakers to oppose it. The repression caused by living as a Pole, as Schmitt quoted, had strengthened Polish cohesion, which was contrary to government's intentions.

This type of national consciousness was limited to the upper strata of society during the first half of the 19th century. However, as repression began to extend to the inner life of individuals from the second half of the 19th century to the 20th century, national cohesion and consciousness spread to a much broader segment of society. This consciousness eventually led to the Wielkopolska uprising from December 27, 1918 to February 16, 1919, immediately after World War I. As a result of this uprising, it was decided that the entire province of Posen would be part of Poland before the Paris Peace Conference in 1919. This course was different from those followed by the provinces of East Prussia, West Prussia, and Silesia after World War I, which were generally divided between Germany and Poland. This was a consequence of Polish consciousness spreading through the province of Posen.

The Wielkopolska uprising became a memory of victory and success for the Polish people in Posen. At the same time, it has become the starting point for a new narrative unique to the region and will continue to create differences from other regions[20].

References

Amtsblatt der Königlich Preußischen Regierung zu Bromberg /Dziennik Urzędowy Królewsko Pruskiéy Regencyi w Bydgoszczy. (abbreviated as *AB*)

Amtsblatt der Königlich Preußischen Regierung zu Posen/ Dziennik Urzędowy Królewskiey Regencyi w Poznaniu. (abbreviated as *AP*)

Bergmann, Eugen [1883]. *Zur Geschichte der Entwickelung deutscher, polnischer und jüdischer Bevölkerung in der Provinz Posen seit 1824* Tübingen: Verlag der H. Laupp'schen Buchhandlung.

Richard Blanke, *Prussian Poland in the German Empire (1871-1900)* (New York, 1981),

Böckh, Richard [1894]. Die Verschiebung der Sprachverhältnisse in Posen und Westpreussen, *Preussische Jahrbücher* 77, pp. 424-436.

Gesetzsammlung für die Königlichen Preußischen Staaten (abbreviated as *GS*)

Korth, Rudolf [1963]. *Die preussische Schulpolitik und die polnischen Schulstreiks: ein Beitrag zur preußischen Polenpolitik der Ära Bülow.* Würzburg: Holzner.

Kopp, Kristin [2012]. *Germany's Wild East: Constructing Poland as Colonial Space.* Ann Arbor: University of

---

[20] For example, as a special feature of the 100th anniversary of the Wielkopolska uprising, see: *Kronika Miasta Poznania* 3/2018. [*1918. Od powstania do rewolucji.*]

Michigan Press.

Kronika Miasta Poznania 3/2018. [*1918. Od powstania do rewolucji.*] Poznań: Wydawnictwo Miejskie Poznania.

Kulczycki, John J. [1981]. *School strikes in Prussian Poland, 1901-1907: the struggle over bilingual education*. New York: Columbia university press.

Namier, L.B. [1946]. *1848: The Revolution of the Intellectuals*. London: Oxford University Press.

Perdelwitz, Richard [1936]. *Die Posener Polen von 1815-1914. Ein Jahrhundert großpolnischer Ideenge-schichte*. Schneidemühl: Comenius=Buchhandlung.

Preußische Gesetzsammulung.

Preussische Statistik, Bd.209. Heft.3 [1908].

Schmidt, Hans [1912]. *Die polnische Revolution des Jahres 1848*. Weimar: Alexander Duncker Verlag.

Wehler, Hans-Ulrich [1973]. *Das Deutsche Kaiserreich 1871-1918*. Gottingen: Vandenhoeck & Ruprecht.

Authors and organizers of the coference

Jacek Izydorczyk (Ambassador of the Republic of Poland in Japan)

 Jacek Izydorczyk specializes in criminal law, international criminal procedure, criminology, international law comparative law. He has over 100 scientific publications, including in English and Japanese. He graduated from the Faculty of Law at the University of Lódź in 1996. He became a lecturer there the following year. In 2005 he passed judge's national exam. He studied at Kyushu University (2005-2007). In 2011 he became a Professor of Law, and in 2013 a Head of Department of Special Criminal Proceedings. On 9 February 2017 he was appointed as Poland's ambassador to Japan. On 24 May 2017 he presented the letter of credence to the Emperor Akihito. He ended his term on 31 July 2019. He was a member of polish swimming national team (1978-1991). Publication: 'The rule of legalism (mandatory prosecution) in Polish criminal law', *Journal of law and politics* (Faculty of Law Kyushu University, 73-4, 2007).

Zdzisław Krasnodębski (Professor, University of Bremen)

Zdzisław Krasnodębski graduated from the Faculty of Philosophy and Sociology at the University of Warsaw and in 1981 from the Ruhr -Universität Bochum. In 1984 he obtained a PhD at the University of Warsaw. From 1976 to 1991, he taught sociology, social theory and philosophy at the University of Warsaw. From 1991-1992 he was a professor at the University of Kassel. In 1992 he settled in Germany. In 1995 he was appointed professor at the University of Bremen. He was appointed to the Committee the Sociology of the Polish Academy of Sciences (1999-2006). In 2018-2019, he was a Vice President of the European Parliament. Major Publications: *Upadek idei postępu* (Ośrodek Myśli Politycznej, 2009), *Postmodernistyczne rozterki kultury* (INNE, 1996), *M. Weber* (WP, 1999), *Demokracja peryferii* (Słowo obraz terytoria, 2005)

Akiko Kasuya (Professor, Kyoto City University of Arts): Moderator

Akiko Kasuya was born in Hyogo in 1963. She studied aesthetics in the Institute of Aesthetics at Jagiellonian University from 1989 to 1991. She graduated from Division of Philosophy in the Graduate School of Letters at Kyoto University (Doctoral Program) in 1991. She has worked at the Curatorial Department of the National

Museum of Art, Osaka (NMAO) from 1991. Her major exhibitions at NMAO include Art and The Environment (1998), Miroslaw Balka—Between Meals (2000), A Second Talk (2002); Positioning-In the New Reality of Europe (2005); Still/Motion: Liquid Crystal Painting (2008); Homage to Kantor – Theater of Death (2015); Tatsuno Art Project 2011-2016 etc. She joined the faculty at Kyoto City University of Art in 2008. Major Publications: *Modern Art in Central Europe* (Co-author, Sairyusha, 2013), *Contemporary Art of Central Europe* (Co-author, Sairyusya, 2014), *Polish Avant-garde Art: Applied Fantasy for Survival* (Sogensha, 2014).

Tokimasa Sekiguchi (Honorary professor, Tokyo University of Foreign Studies): Commentator

 He graduated from the Faculty of Letters at the University of Tokyo. In 1979, he completed the master's program in Comparative Literature and Culture, Graduate School of Art and Humanities at the University of Tokyo. He studied at Jagiellonian University as a scholarship student financed by Polish government. From 1992 to 2013, he worked at Tokyo University of Foreign Studies. At present he is a Professor Emeritus at Tokyo University of Foreign Studies. He received the 69th Yomiuri Prize for Literature (Research/Translation Award) and the 4th Best Translation Award for translation of *Lalka* by Bolesław Prus (Michitani, 2017). Major books: *Poland and others* (Misuzu Shobo,), *Eseje nie całkiem polskie* (Universitas, Kraków). Major translations: J. Kochanowski *Elegie*

(Michitani), A. Mickiewicz *Ballad and Romance* (Michitani), S. I. Witkiewicz *Four Dramas of Witkacy* (Michitani), J. Iwaszkiewicz *Mother Joan of the Angels* (Iwanami Shoten), J. Kott *Sketch for a biography* (Misuzu Shobo), Cz. Miłosz "History of Polish Literature" (co-translation, Michitani) *The Complete Letters of Chopin 1816-1830 – Period in Poland* (co-translation, Iwanami Shoten), S. Lem, *Hospital of the Transfiguration* (Kokusho Kankokai), and others.

Kumiko Haba (Professor, Aoyama Gakuin University)

Kumiko Haba is a professor of International Politics at Aoyama Gakuin University in Tokyo. Her research is International Relations, International Politics, Power Shift and National Anxiety, Immigrants-Refugee questions, Nationalism and Xenophobia in the European Union. She graduated from Tsuda College, was Professor at Hosei University (1985–2007), Visiting Scholar at Harvard University (2011–12), European University Institute (2007), Sorbonne University (2004), University of London (1996-1997), and Hungarian Academy of Science, Institute of History (1995–1996). She was a Vice President of International Studies Association in the USA (2016–2017), member of Science Council of Japan, Directorate of JPSA (Japan Political Science Association), of JAIR (Japan Association of International Relations), and the General Secretary of JAREES (Japan Association for Russian and East European Studies). She is now President of JAICOWS, Vice President of ISA Asia Pacific, and Directrate of

EUSAJ (EU Studies Association in Japan). She got a Jean Monnet Chair title from the EU in 2005. Major publications: *The Challenge of Expanding Europe*, Chuokoron, 2014, *The Expanding EU and Central Europe* (Iwanami, 1998), *Division and Integration in Europe; Exclusion or Inclusion?* (Chuokoron, 2016), and others.

Hikaru Ogura (Assistant professor, Toyo University)

 Hikaru Ogura specializes in Russian literature, Polish literature and comparative literature. She graduated from Graduate School of Humanities and Social Sciences at the University of Tokyo with a major in European and American Studies, and obtained a PhD (Literature). In 2001-2002, she was a lecturer at the Faculty of Oriental Studies, Warsaw University. She studied as a researcher at the University of Tokyo Graduate School in 2010-17. Since 2017, she has been an associate professor at Toyo University. She translated the work of Olga Tokarczuk: *Dom dzienny, dom nocny* (Hiruno ie, yoru no ie, Hakusui-sha, 2010), *Bieguni* (Tou bou ha, Hakusui-sha, 2014). Major publications: 'О восточном мышлении в творчестве Ольги Токарчук (On eastern thinking in the works of Olga Tokarczuk)' (*Славянский альманах* 2016. Вып. 3–4), and others.

Motoki Nomachi (Professor, Hokkaido University)

 Motoki Nomachi graduated from the Graduate School of Humanities and Social Sciences at the University of Tokyo with a degree in Western Culture Studies (Slav), and obtained a Ph.D. In 2003-05, he taught as a lecturer at the Faculty of Oriental Studies at Warsaw University. In 2008, he became an associate professor of the Slavic Research Center at Hokkaido University, and in 2017 he became a professor. He specializes in analysis of grammatical structures in the Slavic languages from the viewpoints of language typology, language contact (areal linguistics), and historical linguistics. He has been interested in and intensively studying grammatical changes in minority Slavic languages, focusing particularly on Kashubian, which is spoken mainly in Pomeranian Voivodeship in the northern part of Poland. Major publications: *The Palgrave Handbook of Slavic Languages, Identities and Borders* (Co-author, Palgrave MacMillan, 2016), S*lavic Microphilology* (Co-author, Slavic-Eurasian Research Center, 2018), *Linguistic Regionalism in Eastern Europe and Beyond: Minority, Regional and Literary Microlanguages* (Co-author, Peter Lang, 2018), and others.

Taku Okazaki (Assistant professor, Tokiwa University)

 Taku Okazaki graduated from Kobe University. He completed a doctoral course of the Graduate School of Economics at Kobe University: Ph.D. (Economics). In 2015-2018, he was a part-time lecturer at Shitennoji University. From 2018, he is an assistant professor at the Tokiwa University. He specializes in car industry of East European countries. He analyzes the historical development and structural changes of the Polish automobile industry. Major publications: 'The Development Path of the Automotive Industry in Poland'. *Japanese Journal of Comparative Economics* (53-2, 2016) , 'The Development Strategies of Poland and the Engine of Polish Economic Growth', *Okayama Economic Review* (51-2/3, Co-author, 2020).

Masahiro Taguchi (Professor, Okayama University/ Professor, SGH Warsaw School of Economics)

 Masahiro Taguchi was graduated from the Central School of Planning and Statistics in Warsaw (SGPiS, now SGH Warsaw School of Economics) with a master's degree in economics. He completed a doctoral program of the Graduate School of Economics at Kyoto University. In 1990, he became an associate professor in the Faculty of Liberal Arts at Okayama University. He worked as a visiting researcher in the Center for European Studies (CES) at

Harvard University (1992-1993) and as a visiting professor at the Polish Academy of Sciences (PAN) (1993-1994). He is now a professor in the Graduate School of Humanities and Social Sciences at Okayama University. He is also a professor of the World Economy Research Institute at SGH Warsaw School of Economics. He specializes in transition economics and economic policy. His research areas are modern economic history of Poland and Polish economic policy theory. Major publications: *Political Economy of Transition in Poland. Political Economy of System Collapse and Generation* (Ochanomizu-shobo, 2005), *Modern Polish Economic Development Theory, Political Economy of Growth and Crisis* (Okayama University Faculty of Economics, 2013), and others.

Satoshi Warita (Professor, Aoyama Gakuin University)

Satoshi Warida graduated from the Graduate School of Letters at Aoyama Gakuin University, and obtained a Ph.D. in 2004. He was an associate professor of Miyagi Gakuin Women's University in 2006-2012. In 2012, he became an associate professor of the Department of History in the Faculty of Letters at Aoyama Gakuin University. He became a professor in 2017.

He specializes in the modern history of Prussian = German Poland. Major publications: *State, Nation, Region of Prussia in 1815-1848* (Yushisha Publishing, 2012), 'German language of Province Posen. Thinking about lost language in historical regions', *Empire, People, Language. From the Perspective of Periphery* (eds. Hirata, Hara) (Sangensha, 2017).

On the Identity of Poles

International Scientific Conference on the Occasion
of the 100th Anniversary of Regaining Independence
of the Republic of Poland

2020 年 4 月 30 日　初版発行

編 著 者　　田口　雅弘

発　　行　　ふくろう出版
〒700-0035　岡山市北区高柳西町 1-23
友野印刷ビル
TEL：086-255-2181
FAX：086-255-6324
http://www.296.jp
e-mail：info@296.jp
振替　01310-8-95147

印刷・製本　　友野印刷株式会社
ISBN978-4-86186-784-2 C3030　ⓒ2020
定価は表紙に表示してあります。乱丁・落丁はお取り替えいたします。